CANCER WARRIOR

CANCER WARRIOR

My Passport Back to the Kingdom of the Well

Valerie Ruelos Magalong

Rev. date: 10/19/2021

To order additional copies of this book, contact:
Xlibris
844-714-8691
www.Xlibris.com
Orders@Xlibris.com
835633

In loving memory of my mom.
May your memory be forever held in the pages of this book.
You are forever in my heart.

INTRODUCTION

Celebrating my fifth anniversary of complete remission from cancer didn't look how I thought it would. Typically, I would gather family and friends for a big celebration, with lots of Filipino food, a cover band playing music that we can sing all the words to, or a DJ playing our favorite old-school jams, accompanied by our tone-deaf singing and dances that would date us—like the running man. Or maybe I'd celebrate by planning a vacation somewhere I've always wanted to explore—like Greece or the Maldives—sipping on the locals' drink of choice while checking out all the wonderful culture and sights the country has to offer. Traveling is one of my passions and something I've always made a priority in my life. But as my anniversary coincided with the Covid-19 pandemic of 2020, the trips and gatherings would just have to wait. What that year gave me, unexpectedly, was an opportunity to look back on the past five years while celebrating in a quiet and more reflective way.

This isn't a first for me. Putting things on hold and learning to pivot is something I've gotten good at, and I've even learned how to put a positive spin on it most of the time. My diagnosis of stage 3A colon cancer put everything—work, travel, independence over my life—on pause as I went through chemotherapy for six months. And then shortly after my own treatment wrapped up, my dad was diagnosed with esophageal cancer. Our family, once again, banded together and kicked into gear, shifting our focus from celebrating my recovery to preparing for his treatments. But right before he was to start his battle, our family was asked to endure the unthinkable. On my forty-fifth birthday, my mom, who had unwaveringly supported me through not only my treatment but also my entire life, unexpectedly and suddenly, passed away.

So while I found myself wanting to acknowledge the milestone of my remission, I also found myself just as urgently needing to honor her passing, as well as getting involved in and prepared for my father's cancer journey.

It was during the Covid-19 pandemic that I came across a book that mentioned that the *New York Times* conducted a survey asking people if they wanted to write a book, and 85 percent of those who responded said yes. With the Covid-19 pandemic in full throttle, limiting the celebrations I had planned, I, once again, pivoted and took this opportunity of putting pen to paper to honor my mother as well as to celebrate my dad and me being in remission, and thank all my family and friends for their help during such a hard time in my life.

As I reflected, there were a lot of questions that plagued me as a resident of the kingdom of the sick and as a visitor during my dad's treatment that helped me understand my journey retrospectively. I was able to find peace exploring questions like "Why me?" "What if?" and "What now?"

I know about hard times, and this pandemic was difficult for everyone, but if you can just make it to the next day while staying grateful for the past and looking forward to the future, it does get better. Thinking back to all the amazing people I met along my cancer journey and their strength through their own battles left me in awe—not to mention all the people battling sickness in this current pandemic. For them, may the kingdom of the well prevail, and may they all have family and friends who stand beside them through their journey, just as I had.

Everyone has a story—this is just mine. I hope you find strength and gratitude through life's journey through your own story, and if you find yourself in the kingdom of the sick, may you come out even stronger in the kingdom of the well.

PART I

Passport to the Kingdom of the Well

Everyone who is born holds dual citizenship, in the kingdom of the well and in the kingdom of the sick. Although we all prefer to use the good passport, sooner or later each of us is obliged, at least for a spell, to identify ourselves as citizens of that other place.

—**Susan Sontag,** *Illness as Metaphor*

CHAPTER 1

"I believe you have cancer."

Those words, spoken to me in the recovery room after I woke up from my colonoscopy, still ring through in my head to this day.

It's one of those distressing memories I can never forget, forever burned into my memory. It felt, in a word, paralyzing. Everything I had learned in my forty-four years of life came to a head that day. The past was played out in my mind in short snippets of memories as future plans were put on hold and more important health issues were suddenly forced to the front of the hierarchy of needs. Values and beliefs were put to the test. Ultimately, there are no plans without life itself.

Growing up as a first-generation-born American comes with some pressure. After all, my grandparents and parents gave up their lives in the Philippines and Hawaii and traveled a few thousand miles to provide a better future for their family. This view of a better future included putting family first, being part of a Catholic church community, having a college education, working hard, getting married, having a successful career—and being kind. These values and beliefs were instilled and molded by my grandparents and parents when I was just a child growing up in the San Francisco Bay Area. As part of a hard-working middle-class Filipino family, I wanted to make them all proud and knew that if I followed their blueprint in life, I might find success as well as fulfilling their "American Dream" for future generations. All in all, I was pretty compliant with their asks of me, which helped me mold my own set of values and beliefs.

My dad, Vincent Ruelos Jr., was born in the Philippines during World War II. He was the second-eldest son in his family of eventually five siblings—three boys and two girls. Shortly after his first birthday, the family, which, at this time, just consisted of my grandparents, my oldest uncle, and my dad, all immigrated to Kauai to get away from the perils of war and find work, as jobs in the Philippines was scarce. My grandfather found work in the sugarcane fields in Hawaii, while my grandmother stayed at home to take care of my uncle and my dad. It was during their decade in Hawaii that the family grew and my two aunties and youngest uncle were born.

Shortly after having their last child in Hawaii, my grandparents decided to move their family of seven to the mainland of the United States to find more opportunities for work. They settled on San Francisco as they had some family in the area. My grandma took full advantage of the opportunities in the United States and put herself through what was known back then as beautician school, now known as cosmetology school. My grandparents worked very hard to support their family and in due course ended up owning their own house and a successful beauty salon, both in the Mission District of San Francisco. The salon was where my cousins and I used to work in the summer. Cheap labor for my grandma and free babysitting for our parents! Boy, did we have fun spending time with one another—those were such carefree days. Sure, we worked a little, but we mostly enjoyed one another's company in the salon and running errands with my grandma along the 24th and Mission corridors. Everyone knew Barbara Ruelos, owner of Rose's Beauty Salon—we could not walk an entire block without running into one of her friends, and she would proudly introduce us. My grandfather, in addition to owning the beauty salon with my grandma, also held many jobs providing for his family. To say they were hardworking was an understatement, and they passed along this strong work ethic to my dad.

Once the Ruelos family arrived from Hawaii, my dad attended schools in San Francisco, including Everett Middle School and Galileo High School. Soon after his high school graduation, he joined the Navy. "Go Navy!" was a frequently-uttered phrase throughout my childhood. He boxed for the Navy, and apparently, he was pretty good—he won a lot of tournaments and had a lot of trophies to show for it. I remember watching the Muhammed Ali and Sugar Ray Leonard boxing matches with him when I was younger, and he enjoyed discussing the sport with me— it was obvious it was an important part of his past. He used to tell my mom that he was teaching me how to roller-skate in the garage, while in actuality, he was teaching me uppercut and jab boxing combinations.

My dad spoke about how disciplined the Navy made him and what a difference it made in his life, so it made sense that he provided strong discipline to us growing up. (But he doesn't get all the credit—my mom was even more strict!) He wasn't a strict disciplinarian in the sense of having us do one hundred push-ups on our knuckles at 5:00 a.m., but he could certainly be tough. He would teach us to wake up early and be productive about our day and to be detail-oriented in all that we do. As he would say, "Do it right, or just don't do it at all," meaning, if you are going to do something, just don't give it minimal effort—give it everything you've got. After a successful six years of service in the Navy, during which he visited the East Coast and traveled internationally to Vietnam, he came back home to San Francisco where he met my mom in, of all places, my grandmother's beauty salon! Over the years, I have heard stories that my grandma had a hand in setting them up, but I like to think that it was a little bit of that as well as fate.

As for my mom, Leticia Garcia Ruelos was born in the Philippines and traveled to San Francisco by herself in her early twenties in hopes of having more opportunities in America. As I grew older, I admired her for moving to another country and starting her life on her own, as this was something I knew I wouldn't have been able to do in my early adulthood. As my grandma was a schoolteacher in the Philippines, my grandparents instilled the importance of education into their family. They were able to put all eight of their children, including my mom, through college. She graduated from Far Eastern University in the Philippines with a mechanical engineering degree. At that time, it wasn't common for women to attend college, but my mom was very independent and decided to pursue an education in a mainly male-dominated field. Shortly after graduation, she brought her ambition, hopes, and dreams to America. She was the first of all her siblings to arrive in the United States. Her attributes of being educated and strong-willed matched perfectly with my dad's strong work ethic and discipline. Not only were my parents perfect for each other, just as my grandma and grandpa before them, but a sense of adventure was also a common theme, from my mom moving all the way from the Philippines to live in a new country to my dad and his Navy days. Together, they were a force to be reckoned with—my brother and I didn't stand a chance!

One of their first adventures together was the journey to purchase their first home. Their real estate goal came to fruition in 1970. With all their hard work and money saved, they were able to purchase their first home in San Francisco. A year later, I was born, and five years later, my brother, Brandon, was born. Because of my parents' hard work and a desire to stay true to their core values, my parents were able to put my brother and me through a Catholic grade school education. My brother attended St. Peter's Catholic School in the Mission District, and I went to St. Gabriel's Catholic School in the Sunset.

My dad worked at Pacific Bell in San Leandro, California, for most of his career. It was a job that he had to commute across the Bay Bridge to every day for twenty-five years. He would wake up at 5:00 a.m. every day and come home around 4:00 p.m. Like all San Francisco Bay Area locals of the era, we have a memorable story around the Loma Prieta earthquake of 1989. We had quite a scare around the collapse of the eastern span of the Bay Bridge. My dad was supposed to be on the bridge at the time of the collapse, but by the grace of God, he left work early that day to avoid the traffic around the local World Series game that was to be played that evening. I remember rushing home from my first semester in college and running into the kitchen. The relief that washed over me when I saw him making a sandwich gave way to pure joy. My mom had left work early that day too in hopes that she would find him at home, and when she found us, including my brother, in the kitchen eating sandwiches, he turned to her and said, "What took you so long? Want a sandwich?" It was one of those stress-relieving laughs we all needed.

He eventually retired after twenty-five years at Pacific Bell, but he didn't stop working. Soon after, he took on another job repairing ATMs for banks as supplemental income, and when my mom retired, she went along on the drives, especially the ones that took my dad up and down the Northern California Coast. They would tell me all about all the enjoyable lunches and adventures they had exploring the coastal towns.

Like every married couple, my parents had their differences, but they were able to work it out because their core values remained the same, their differences balanced each other out, and they encouraged each other's personal growth. They were very humble and never discussed their success as a couple, and I remember when my mom wanted to learn about the real estate business and my dad encouraged her to get her real estate license. She would go to work during the day, and my dad, my brother, and I would pick her up at night from her real estate classes. All her hard work paid off, and she obtained her license with my dad's encouragement. I can still hear my mom's advice, "Not everyone is perfect, Val. You just have to find the perfect person for you."

As for me, born and raised in the San Francisco Bay Area and the eldest of two siblings, I felt the pressure to always succeed, whether it was in school or in my own personal life. It's an Asian culture thing, and my family would always tell me, "You have to set an example for your brother!" It was meant as encouragement to consistently do the right thing, but I felt the pressure. I took it lightheartedly and really didn't step out of line too much. My parents were pretty strict, and being a parent now, I totally get it! It must have been hard for my mom raising children in a country that is foreign to you—I know that, for me, it would be pretty damn scary, but she always said you have to have faith. Her faith and love were always at the heart of our family.

We went to church every Sunday when we were growing up, and I still can picture her getting mad at us for fidgeting around in the pews. An hour can be a long time for a child to sit and pay attention. There was a time I tried to challenge her about Sunday mass, saying, "Mom, I attend mass at school once a week for an hour! Doesn't that count for going to church for the week?"

She was always quick, stern, and a bit witty with her responses, almost as if she knew what I was going to ask her. Her reply to me was, "Val, God gave you twenty-four hours today. Don't you think two hours a week isn't a lot to give back to Him?"

See what I mean? Who could argue with that reasoning? And with that, I put on my best Sunday clothes and went to church with her and tried not to fidget.

The Catholic faith was instilled in my brother and me since birth. We were both baptized within six months of being born and received most of the sacraments growing up. My mom was adamant that my brother and I be raised with a core spiritual belief, and I'm glad she did; it has helped me overcome some of my most difficult moments, especially when my dad and I were going through our health issues. Although I'm not a practicing Catholic, I drew from that faith to get through those dark times.

Education was also very important to my parents, especially my mom. Being college-educated, she understood the value and opportunities it brought to her as a female immigrant in the United States. "Education, along with faith," she always said, "will help us be successful in life and help us through tough times." There was no option for me whether to attend college or not, I knew I had to, and when I was little, I looked forward to going someday. This is where I believed she instilled those values—"Dream big!" she used to say to me. She understood that a woman with a degree still faces many challenges, but with faith and an educated mind, it can only help. Again, she was right! After all, she was one of the few women to graduate from her college with a mechanical engineering degree, typically a male-dominated major.

Grade school was full of happy memories—I had so much fun. I basically went to school with the same people from kindergarten to eighth grade, so I guess you can say we all grew up together! All our families knew one another, and it was a tight-knit community. Even during this time, my mom kept me focused on the next step. "Look further, Val. What high school do you want to go to?" This was a trick question as I already knew she wanted me to try to get into one of the most prestigious public high schools in San Francisco, Lowell High School. Being so young and not really knowing what high school I wanted to go to, I took my parents' advice and set my goal to get into Lowell. Getting into Lowell meant maintaining my current 4.0 GPA, along with being a part of extracurricular activities. Studies came easy to me during middle school, and I enjoyed being on the volleyball team as well as the cheerleading squad, so at times I felt the goal was attainable.

During my eighth-grade year, I applied to Lowell, and I was accepted! My parents could not have been prouder. I remember receiving the letter in the mail and my mom hugging me so hard after I read the acceptance letter out loud to her. She smiled at me and said, "Now the real work begins!" That's my mom, always thinking ahead, attaining a goal, celebrating it, and on to the next goal. I was way too young and excited to even think of the next goal. I was stuck on the celebrating aspect and looking forward to my eighth-grade graduation party with all my family.

We were a tight-knit family, and growing up, my cousins were my first best friends. We would spend weekends at my grandma and grandpa's house in the Mission District with all of my dad's side of the family, including all my aunts, uncles, and cousins—it could be upwards of thirty people every weekend. So when it came time for celebrations, the parties were epic. The amount of food alone was enough to feed a small wedding, and I suppose it made sense, as there were upwards of sixty of us, including close family friends, at our celebrations. There would be trays of Filipino food, including pancit (a noodle dish similar to chow mein), adobo (marinated meat), lechon (roasted pig), and countless other dishes lining the dining room table and even spilling over to the kitchen counters—with another table solely dedicated to desserts. There would be a bar for the adults and a soda table for the kids. The men would partake in a family game of blackjack, while the women would play mahjong (an Asian tile-based game). We kids kept ourselves busy by riding our bikes, roller-skating, playing hide-and-go-seek, or just hanging out, telling one another stories while bonding. With such a big extended family, it can get hectic, but it was always exciting and fun, and I wouldn't have it any other way.

Lowell High School was *hard!* For the first time, I felt I had to step up my game. Before high school, I would always get great grades—it came easy for me. I would look over schoolwork the night before a test and get an A without developing any strong study habits. Now in high school, I would have to study hard to just get a passing grade! Lowell High School is very competitive, and I remember students crying in the hallway after receiving an A-. A lot of pressure was put on the students to receive a 4.0 grade point average or even higher—yes, it's possible to get higher than a 4.0 by taking advanced placement classes. I was constantly studying because I didn't want to let my mom and dad down, and eventually, I buckled down and picked up some study habits from the "A students" and graduated from Lowell all while holding down a part-time job.

That's another reason I studied hard: to keep my part-time job. My mom had threatened me that if my grades slipped, I would have to quit. My parents afforded my brother and me with everything we needed, but growing up in the 80s, I wanted to buy "cooler" things, like cassette tapes, those trendy 80s clothes, and have extra gas money.

After high school, I attended City College of San Francisco for two years, earning my AA degree, and then transferred to San Francisco State University. College was just so much easier for me than high school—maybe because I had refined my study habits! Also, in college, I was able to take classes for my major that I was actually interested in, so it made it easier for me to learn.

I breezed through college in four years, earning my Bachelor of Arts in Communications. San Francisco State University was a fifteen-minute drive from my home, so I would just basically drive to and from school and didn't go to a lot of college parties, so I guess that's part of the reason I graduated in four years. I always wondered what it would have been like going away for college. I wished I had had that experience and told myself that if I ever had kids, I would definitely want them to experience going away for college. But I keep in mind the saying "the grass is always greener on the other side." I don't regret staying close to home for college, as I was able to stay close to my parents and experience all our extended-family celebrations.

I remember my college graduation well—seeing my mom, dad, and brother sitting in the sea of people at SFSU and being able to point them out, their smiles beaming with happiness in the stands. It was such an awesome day to walk the stage and know they were so proud of my accomplishment!

Soon after college, like every new graduate, I tried to find my footing in the world and explored the different career paths that were available to me. One of my first jobs after college was working in a dermatology clinic in San Francisco. In a few years of working there, I was able to learn a lot about the front and back office of a medical private practice. It was, at this time, that my coworker introduced me to Lee.

Lee was a single father who worked as a police officer. He had a four-year-old son named Jeron, who was quite the little charmer. He gave me my first look into motherhood, and I thank them for the opportunity to help raise Jeron. Lee, Jeron, and I dated for about a year before we decided to get married, and Jeron was the cutest ring bearer at our wedding.

I was married at the tender age of twenty-seven and had my son soon after my twenty-ninth birthday. It was Labor Day weekend, and boy did that give a whole new meaning to Labor Day. After being in labor for ten hours, Jett finally decided to arrive—all ten pounds of him! To put it into perspective, I'm five feet, four inches tall and medium build, so a labor of love it was! I remember telling the nurse in the midst of pushing that I just couldn't do it anymore and I was too tired to keep pushing. I promised her that I'd come back tomorrow to finish. Ha! Wishful thinking!

Motherhood was a whole new ballgame for me. I was already a stepmother to Jeron, but he was already four years old when I met him, so being a mother to a newborn baby was damn scary. A few of my friends and cousins had had babies around the same time, so I had the support of others going through the same ups and downs of being a new mother. My parents provided a ton of support too, most likely because they sensed my nervousness and it's a cultural thing to help their children with whatever they can provide. In my case, it was babysitting, as my husband and I were working full-time jobs. My parents, still working themselves, would help pick up Jett from the babysitter and Jeron from school after their own workday had ended. I was commuting across the Bay Bridge, and Lee was working swing shifts as a police officer. By the time I got home, the kids had finished eating dinner, and Jeron was halfway done with his homework. I was so grateful to have my parents helping us.

My parents even assisted us with a down payment for our first home together, and I am still fortunate to live in the home that they helped me buy. They oversaw the construction of this brand-new house, and we appreciated all their insight and experience as property owners.

Years prior, my mom and dad had owned a four-unit apartment building, and they managed all the maintenance on it themselves. And as a result, my brother and I learned how to be handy. I remember my dad would get calls late at night, saying a pipe had burst, and my parents would leave to attend to it.

Their American dream of owning property manifested, and so they wanted us to experience the pride of real estate ownership too. And in keeping with the theme of the importance of family, the property they put a down payment on was a duplex, in hopes that one day when my brother was married, he would live right next door to me. Eventually, my brother did get married, and he and his wife, Shana, moved in next door to us, and I am lucky enough to see them and my handsome nephew Riley and beautiful niece Reese on a daily basis. My parents live only fifteen minutes away, and they would come over often. So even as we formed our own families, we remained a tight-knit family, spending weekends together to eat and hang out.

Up to this point in my life, things had seemed pretty effortless. I mean, getting straight A's in elementary and middle school and then getting into the high school of my (well, my mom's) choice was uncomplicated. Sure, there were struggles in high school, but I got through them, and with the study habits I had learned at Lowell, it made college seem like a walk in the park. Married life was going well, and we were raising two handsome and happy boys with the help of my mom and dad. The only thing missing at this point in my life was a career with some kind of purpose, something that I felt passionate about. At this point, I had left the dermatology office and was working at a television station in the Bay Area. It was a great job in the sales department and came with many perks. I was able to take the boys to see many free events that they were interested in at the time, like the circus, monster truck shows, ball games (in the network suite), and all the Bay Area amusement parks. And because I was working full time, I had the security of my own benefits and building my 401K—but there was something still missing, some need to be fulfilled. My career path needed to find its purpose, and I was willing to put in the time and effort to find it. Little did I know, life would have some changes in store for me.

CHAPTER 2

Up until now, everything seemed like it was falling into place in my life. By twenty-nine years old, I was married with two handsome and happy boys, and I even had a house of my own, but I could tell something was brewing as challenges started to arise in my marriage. We found ourselves starting to bicker about little things. Then in 2007, it all came to a screeching halt— my marriage was starting to unravel. *Change* is a word with which I would get all too comfortable. To get adept at adjusting to change, I had to learn to focus my energy not on fighting the old ways but building up a new path for myself.

Early on in our marriage, I was working at a local Bay Area TV station, where I met some pretty amazing girlfriends with whom I remain close. Once a year, we would go on a girls' trip to Vegas. Sure, we did the clubbing thing, but the best memories were made watching games in the sportsbook area of the casinos and trying our luck on parlays. We were a sporty bunch who knew our way around sports-betting and loved watching all the games.

One friendship from that period that I still cherish to this day is with Samantha, who has been my best friend for over twenty years. We are so close that she could probably write this book about me—I'm glad she isn't! Going through life's ups and downs is always easier when you have a best friend at your side to share those moments with. We had a great time working at the TV station, spending weekends at concert venues and sports arenas. But I knew it wouldn't be sustainable for my marriage if I continued that path as my weekends were spent at work events and not at home with my family and newborn son. So I decided that I needed a different career path.

During my time as a police officer's wife, I met a friend, Ingrid, who was also married to an officer. She worked at a big biotechnology company in the Bay Area that was always on *Fortune's* list of the one hundred best companies to work for. I would always hear great stories about what this company does for cancer and immunology patients and all the breakthrough drugs they created. I know it sounds corny, but their mission really spoke to me. I wanted to be part of a company that helps patients, so I asked her if there were any openings that would be a fit with my degree and background. As it was a biotechnology company, I assumed that someone with a Bachelor of Science would be a preferred candidate, but I was willing to start anywhere to work for this company. She sent me some descriptions of open positions, I applied, and with her help, I was able to land an interview. The process started with a phone interview, and once I got beyond that, I faced a grueling panel interview with the eight directors of the department. I had to wait two weeks after my interview to find out the outcome. It was exactly two weeks after my last interview when I finally received the call and I was offered a position at the company. I don't think I thanked her enough for helping me, so I'd like to say thank you, Ingrid, for taking a chance on me! I was ecstatic to work for such a distinguished company that valued patients and their employees.

One of the many fabulous perks this company offered was paying partly for me to attend graduate school. While I got my legs under me in my new role, I found myself wondering if this is something I could do—I remember feeling excited by the prospect of that challenge. After all, the importance of education was one of the cornerstones of how I was raised. One day at work, I went out to lunch with my coworker, Maia, who later became a very close friend. Maia asked me, "Have you ever thought about getting your MBA?"

My reply, "Every day."

I took this conversation as a sign. She went on to tell me that she had been interested in it too, so during that lunch, we made plans to visit a few local Bay Area colleges to get more information about their MBA programs.

Two weeks after our initial lunch conversation, we enrolled in the University of San Francisco's Executive MBA program. It's always easier to do something with a friend, and grad school was definitely no different—in fact, I recommend it. It's not so bad when you have a friend to bounce ideas off of, give you pep talks during the grueling hours of studying, reading endless case studies, and exploring the causes of underlying principles.

This decision meant a lot of sacrifices for my family. The classes were scheduled all day every Saturday for eighteen months, which meant I had to be away from my family. Since Lee sometimes works weekends, I would have to ask my parents to watch the kids. As it was for my education, my parents didn't seem to mind too much and supported me by helping watch the kids. My mom did warn me, "I know you are having some problems in your marriage, and you have to give that attention too."

I told her, "Don't worry, Mom. I have it under control."

I actually had a great time during my eighteen-month MBA program, and I looked forward to attending class every Saturday. My plate was pretty full as I was raising two kids, trying to keep my marriage together, attending graduate school, and juggling a new career, but soon after my 2009 graduation from the MBA program, it became apparent that my husband and I had grown apart and divorce was inevitable.

In addition to being on my own without my partner, I had the comfort and security of a two-income household suddenly taken away. My ex-husband did provide his share for the kids, but I now had to provide for myself as well as my son. I had to figure out how to pay a mortgage and household bills on a single income. To add to that, as with any Catholic Asian family, I was brought up knowing that once you get married, divorce is not an option—that would bring shame to the entire family. So it was a rough time, to say the least. My parents did let me know their disdain for my divorce, but they also knew that their daughter needed their help. They stayed true to form and were always there for me. They were a *huge* help to Jett and me when it came to the daily routines. I would drop Jett off at their home in the mornings, and they would make him breakfast and take him to school while I went to work. We had our system down: We would wake up at 7:00 a.m., and he would put on his uniform, and I would drop him off around 7:30 a.m. at my mom and dad's house. They would wait at the front gate as he jumped out of the car to greet him, and I wouldn't even have to get out of the car.

I did the best I could as a single mom working full time, but sometimes it meant cutting corners, like feeding Jett sugar-loaded cereal for breakfast—not that he had any complaints. My folks would also pick him up after school, so I wouldn't have to rush between work and picking him up. They would tell me to take my time as Jett's school was close to their home. As the years went by, they also understood how I needed to go out and be with friends, so they became my go-to babysitters—the only ones that Jett ever had. Again, I am so grateful for them.

Because I had so much help with Jett, I was able to focus on work, and now it has been fifteen years that I've been at the biotech company. I had the same manager, Christine, for the first twelve years that I worked there. I was with her longer than I was with my husband, and she has played a huge part in my life, professionally as well as personally. She was one of the greatest managers anyone could have. She understood what I was going through personally while inspiring me to be my best self at work.

I truly enjoy being around Christine. It's her energy and the way she balances work and life that I admire. She had three young children during the time that we worked together, and she made it look effortless, while here I was with one child, barely holding it together. If she wasn't my manager, she would be one of my close friends—you know, the rich one that you make pay for everything! But seriously, I can't stress enough what a positive influence Christine was in my personal life as well as professionally.

While working at the same company for fifteen years, I saw people come and go and move within other departments at the company. If you are lucky, the people you see at work on a daily basis become your extended family—and I was lucky enough to have experienced this. They became my go-to core group for insight, professionally and personally. And because I enjoyed working there so much, I even brought over my BFF Samantha, who had also worked at the television station with me.

We had some fun times and still do! Another one of the special people I met there was Lisa. She worked in the biooncology department, and we kept each other laughing through the good and bad days for many years. Little did I know that she would become instrumental in my cancer journey, as the biooncology department helped develop my chemotherapy medication and she put me in touch with some of the oncology doctors in her department.

I also became familiar with the process of how medicines get approved for use by the Food and Drug Administration (FDA). It's a long process, from a product getting clinically developed to when it finally gets approved for use. I'll try to explain the process simply: First, the medicine is pre-clinically tested in animals, then the sponsor of the drug must show the FDA the results of the preclinical testing in laboratory animals and present what they propose to do for human testing. After that, the drug goes through three phases of human testing, also known as clinical trials. If all goes well with the clinical testing, a new drug application (NDA) is submitted to the FDA. Submitting the NDA is the formal step asking the FDA to consider a drug for marketing approval, and the FDA has sixty days to decide whether to file it for review. Once the NDA is filed, an FDA review team is assigned to evaluate the sponsor's research on the drug's safety and effectiveness. The information is then reviewed for the drug's professional labeling—which is basically information on how to use the drug. As part of the approval process, the FDA also inspects the manufacturing facility where the drug will be produced. If all goes well during this process, the FDA reviewers will approve the application or issue a complete response letter. That's a simplified summary of the process. In the United States, it typically takes over a decade and costs run up into the billions for an experimental drug to arrive onto the pharmacy shelves.

I was learning a lot about the drug development process and surrounding myself with a close circle of friends. Work couldn't be better. But navigating around the whole single-mom life was something I didn't know anything about. It was scary after being out of the dating game for so long! I knew I didn't want to be tied down in a new relationship quickly—I felt I needed some time for myself. Soon after my divorce, I took a trip with some close friends, who also happened to be single. We traveled to Costa Rica, and after that first successful international trip, my best friend Samantha and I decided to add traveling to the seven continents to our bucket list— my parents' spirit of adventure clearly passed down. Our bucket list was one of those aspirational ones, but we figured we would just deal with it one checkmark at a time. Every year we would decide on a different continent, plan the itinerary, pack our bags, and just go and experience a new place while expanding our perspective on the world.

The first new continent that Sam and I traveled to together outside of North America was Europe, and this 2012 adventure was a very special trip, as my mom decided to come with us. Actually, Sam and I invited ourselves on my mom's planned trip with my aunt and their friends. The party started on the plane, with all our collective excitement about traveling to a new country. We flew to Barcelona and stayed there a few days, then boarded a cruise ship and traveled the Mediterranean. Barcelona was so full of splendor and beautiful sights, not to mention delicious food and cava! The most memorable moment for me wasn't touring the beautiful gothic buildings, nor admiring Gaudi's La Sagrada Familia—though all that was breathtaking—but rather sitting in a little restaurant on Las Ramblas with my mom and my best friend eating paella and sipping cava. Well, maybe my mom was the only one doing what could be called sipping. I will always remember the laughs and smiles from that day. After our lunch, we walked around Las Ramblas and watched street performers and eventually found ourselves stumbling into La Boqueria Market. The atmosphere in the market was just as energetic as it was in the street, and the explosive colors of the fresh fruits in the stalls reminded me of fireworks. It's those little moments that make for lasting memories—I cherish the ones from that trip and the subsequent ones.

The following year we set our sights on Australia with the same group of friends that we went with to Costa Rica. There are always at least six of us on these trips as we believe in safety in numbers when traveling to the unknown, but the main reasons are our shared love of adventure and of spending time with friends while experiencing a new country. Never could I ever have imagined myself being in the South Pacific watching the musical *South Pacific* at the Sydney Opera House. On that trip, we also took a side journey to Middle Earth, New Zealand, to see the Shire.

It's such a beautiful country with lush greenery, beautiful beaches, and amazing wineries. My love of travel grew exponentially on that trip, and before it was over, we all agreed that the next continent we wanted to visit would be Africa!

The following year we found ourselves experiencing that beautiful continent. It took us over twenty-four hours to travel to Cape Town, South, Africa from San Francisco, but so worth it, as it is arguably my favorite continent I have visited so far. We went diving with the great white sharks in Gansbaai, close to the southern tip of the continent. Outfitted with only wetsuits and snorkel gear, five of us at a time were lowered in a cage into the shark-infested water. It was just as scary as it sounds, but once we were in the water, our fears subsided, and we became mesmerized by the beauty of these sharks. The next day we found ourselves in awe of more incredible creatures at a safari in Kruger National Park game reserve, where, not to be outdone by the sharks, an elephant charged our Jeep. Luckily, our experienced guide was able to maintain his cool, defusing the situation by backing the Jeep slowly away from the charging elephant.

We also learned a little bit about history as we toured the homes of Nelson Mandela and Bishop Desmond Tutu. We spent one afternoon at the Apartheid Museum, which brought to life for us the rise and fall of apartheid through a moving experience. South Africa was one of my all-time favorite trips, as it proved that it is all about the journey and not the destination— even when the destination is pretty amazing. More memories were made with my traveling group, and I was well on my way to hit the seven continents on my bucket list!

About two months after my Africa trip, I embarked on a new adventure. It's true what they say about meeting that special someone when you least expect it. On December 14, 2014, Sam and I decided to go to dinner in San Francisco, check out the Christmas lights in Union Square, and do a little Christmas shopping. During dinner, I received an instant message on my social media page. Yep, he slid into my DMs!

I'd constantly heard stories about Cisco from two different groups of friends—we ran in the same circles, but we had never met. One of my girlfriends, Carmela, who is also part of my seven-continent travel group, would tell me stories about all the fun they would have when they hung out. She mentioned that I would really get along with him and that she wanted to introduce us. I never took her up on the offer—dating wasn't really that important to me. I thought, if I'm meant to meet him, I will meet him; no need to go out of my way to meet someone, as I was pretty content and busy with my life. My other friends John and Michelle, who I met through Jett's Catholic school and knew for the entire eight years he was there, would also tell me they had a single friend named Cisco, who they thought I would really get along with, and that they thought I should meet. I couldn't get away from hearing about this guy! So I said to myself, why not, it's been five years since I've been divorced. Yes, I'd dated in between then, but for some reason, this felt different—two different sets of trusted friends wanted us to meet each other. I looked at it this way: If we didn't hit it off, then I just found a new friend. And even though I believe guys look at it differently, seeing it as being sent to the friend zone, I thought, "Whatever," and I went ahead and entertained his direct message.

Before I knew it, we were talking to each other on the phone on a daily basis, sometimes up to three times a day, with quick text messages throughout the day. The conversations were so easy. We always had something to say to each other, and we laughed like teenagers, staying up late to talk. Jett asked me one morning who I had been talking to on the phone because he had never heard me laugh so hard. That put a smile on my face—it's important for your child to know that you are happy. After a week of talking, Cisco asked me out to dinner, maybe to see if I was catfishing him. I half had the thought that maybe he was catfishing me, as we'd never seen each other in person at this point and had only seen pictures of each other through our mutual friends and social media. In any case, we would finally be meeting up in person.

I remember that night like it was yesterday. It was December 21, and I met him at Fog Harbor Fish House at Pier 39 in San Francisco for dinner. The pier was beautifully lit up with holiday lights, and you could feel the San Francisco holiday spirit in the air. I talked to Sam on the phone on the way there, telling her I was nervous, and we thought that was weird, as we find it easy to talk to meet people and just have casual conversations. As always, she gave me the best pep talk and said it's just like meeting a new friend, so go meet him! So I walked into the restaurant, and there he was sitting at the table, and I thought to myself, *Yeah, I definitely wasn't catfished.* The holiday lights twinkled around our table, and I greeted him with a hug—by the way, he gave a great hug—and as I glanced down at the table, there was a bottle of wine. Score a point for Cisco. *Here's another test*, I thought. *Let's see what type of wine he ordered*, and I was thrilled to see it was one of my favorites. Score another point for Cisco. He said he didn't know what type of wine to pick but remembered the name of my favorite winery through our conversations and he felt it was a lucky sign when he found it on the menu. The rest of the night could not have gone any smoother, conversations and wine flowed throughout the night, and at the end of dinner, we took a walk to the end of the pier to check out the sea lions in all their glory. We decided we didn't want the night to end yet, so we drove to Ghirardelli Square to have dessert. It was a perfect first date, and I looked forward to the next one.

Everything was coming into place for me at this point in my life. I was finally feeling confident as a single mom. Lee and I had found success in coparenting, and Jett was about to enter a new chapter too, high school. I was embarking on a new relationship with Cisco, and my connection with my parents was stronger than ever. They would even volunteer to help watch Jett when I would go on my trips with my friends—after all, they knew full well where I had inherited that sense of adventure!

I definitely could not have accomplished all I had done in my life so far without my parents' never-ending help and support, for which I am so very grateful. Because of them, I was able to travel with my best friends and experience different places and cultures and meet people all over the world. My travel group was busy planning for our next continent, South America. Things were on an upswing, and my enthusiasm for life was energized, as everything was starting to fall into place—or so I thought.

PART II

A Layover in the Kingdom of the Sick

CHAPTER 3

The year 2015 was shaping up to be a great year, with a brand-new relationship, my ninth work anniversary, and Jett completing his first semester of high school with flying colors. He chose to go to a high school that was closer to our home, one no one from his Catholic school was going to attend, so he had to start all over and make new friends—such a courageous thing to do at that age. I wasn't too worried about him, as he has always been social and made friends quickly. As for me, my relationship with Cisco was going really well, so we decided to take the next step and meet each other's families after four months of dating. Cisco met Jett first, and a few months later, I met his two boys, one the same age as Jett and the other two years older. We spent some date nights with all three boys, going to dinner, watching movies, shopping, going bowling. I was relieved that they all got along and that our families blended nicely together—I'd heard horror stories that it sometimes doesn't go as smoothly with teenagers.

We were only a few months into the new year, and everything was still pretty exciting. Then in April, I started to feel some cramps on the left side of my abdomen. I have a high pain tolerance—I guess pushing out a ten-pound baby will do that to you—so I was able to maintain through the pain for the most part. I chalked it up to "that time of the month" or indigestion, as I had just started a new diet of raw foods and juicing, something that Californians often do. But the pain continued throughout the entire month of May, and by June, the pain became so intense that I found myself doubled-over. I jumped on the Internet, typed in my symptoms, read some articles, and started to self-diagnose. "Hmmm, maybe it's acid reflux or an ulcer, or even worse, diverticulitis!" I had to Google that one. Diverticulitis is basically when your lower intestines become inflamed or infected, which causes severe pain. I started taking over-the-counter medications like Pepcid and Pepto-Bismol, thinking that it would get better in time. It never crossed my mind to see a doctor. I just thought, *I'm always healthy and still pretty young, this too shall pass.* The word *cancer* just never entered my thoughts. I was too busy concentrating on the positives in my life, like preparing Jett to get his driver's license. And to be honest, it's just not in my nature to think that way, that it could even be that bad.

Then one day at work, I had a meeting with my manager, Christine. At that time, the pain I was experiencing was so bad that I started to hold my stomach and cringe in pain. We were just five minutes into the meeting before she started inquiring about what was wrong with me. After working with someone for eleven years, you begin to know all their nuances, and she knew something was wrong. She told me to leave work immediately and have it checked out by a doctor right away. Typically, the pain would pass, but on this particular day, it seemed more intense and frequent, so I drove myself to the hospital. Thankfully, my primary physician had an opening, so I was able to be seen by her that day. I told her my symptoms of excruciating pain in my lower left abdomen and that I was starting to feel faint and nauseated. She made some calls and told me I need to go to the radiology department to get some scans done. Before I knew it, I was in a wheelchair—walking intensified the pain—being whisked away to get a CT scan, with a stop at the lab to get some blood work done.

A CT scan is a computerized tomography (CT) scan that combines a series of X-ray images taken from different angles around your body and uses computer processing to create cross-sectional images (slices) of the bones, blood vessels, and soft tissues inside your body. CT scan images provide more detailed information than X-rays can provide.

It was my first CT scan, and I thought, *It couldn't be that bad.* I'd seen this in movies and TV shows, where you lay on this table on your back and they and put you through a scanner, similar to a moving massage table, but with a circular opening. Pretty simple, I thought. Boy was I wrong! The nurse injected iodine into my arm, which is a special dye that acts as a contrast material necessary to highlight the areas of your body being examined. The contrast material blocks X-rays and appears white on images, which can help emphasize blood vessels, intestines, or other structures. The dye was injected into my body intravenously, and the heat rush it gave was pretty intense for a few seconds, but it felt like forever. It felt like my whole body was going to implode, while the back of my mouth started to water profusely. That was definitely a new sensation but one I would come to know well after having many CT scans.

While lying down after being injected with the iodine, the nurse and tech gave me instructions to follow the prompts on the machine. They said, "The machine will tell you when to breathe and when to hold your breath." I gave them a nervous smile to let them know that I understood, and then they exited the room to start the scan. As I lay there waiting for the machine, I felt overwhelmed, thinking about the possible outcomes of the scan results. I closed my eyes, took a deep breath, and hoped for the best outcome, entirely unaware that as I entered the scan tunnel, I was leaving the kingdom of the well and entering the kingdom of the sick.

After my first CT scan and blood work were completed, the hospital gave me some pain meds and sent me home to wait for my results. They told me that my doctor would give me a call the following day. I was able to take the pain meds and felt a bit better as the pain became tolerable again. To my surprise, my primary care doctor called me that same afternoon to let me know that the CT scan and blood tests showed some abnormalities and that she wanted to do further tests, so she scheduled an emergency colonoscopy two days later.

In the days prior to my colonoscopy procedure, the pains became more intense and painful. It was so severe that I called the advice nurse to see if the colonoscopy could be moved up one day—and I was put on the waiting list. So another first was about to happen, my first colonoscopy. I really didn't know what to expect but was told the preparation is worse than the procedure. After having just experienced the iodine injection for the CT scan, I thought how much worse can drinking this special jug of water be? Wrong again, and another procedure I underestimated!

I was told to only consume clear liquids the day before the colonoscopy, which seemed easy enough—I was in too much pain to have a huge appetite. The tough part of the preparation started at 6:00 p.m., the night before my procedure, when I had to drink sixty-four ounces of a laxative powder mixed with water. The powder said it was lemon-flavored, and I'm sure there were hints of lemon, but it was an unbearable salty taste to me. I was told to drink eight ounces every ten to fifteen minutes until I finished half of the sixty-four ounces. The other half of the drink should be consumed at least four hours before my scheduled arrival time.

The preparation was definitely worse than the procedure, compounded with my preexisting pain. I felt like my whole body was about to explode! The feeling of imminent implosion and explosion in my body within days of each other was almost too much to handle. The night before my colonoscopy was the longest night I ever experienced—I don't think I slept that entire night. They wanted me at the hospital at 7:00 a.m., which meant I had to finish the second half of the laxative drink by 3:00 a.m. I remember being in so much pain with cramps and having to hobble to the bathroom every few minutes because of the effects of the drink cleaning out my colon. I remember counting down the hours I had until the procedure in anticipation that I would finally know what was going on with my body. Luckily, I had Cisco there that night to help talk me through the torment. The pain was so excruciating that I remember just lying on the floor in my room because I didn't have the energy to jump in and out of bed. Cisco brought two pillows and a blanket down to the floor where we ended up sleeping, and I remember closing my eyes while he rubbed my back, trying to console me as I attempted to sleep.

The morning of the procedure, I felt exhausted from all the craziness of the preparation and the pain, but now a new layer of uncertainty started to unfold. The procedure itself started to scare me. What if something went wrong? I quickly had to reset my mind: I envisioned that the procedure would go well and that at the end of it, I would know exactly what was wrong with me, and they would give me some type of antibiotics or another medication, and in a few days, I would feel better.

I tried to get in the right frame of mind to deal with all the uncertainty and be hopeful.

I remember lying on a gurney that morning and being wheeled into the waiting area. They let me know that I had the first procedure of the day, so it wouldn't be too long of a wait before they wheeled me into the procedure room. I sat up halfway and took a look around and saw six areas for other patients in the pre-surgery room. It soothed me to know that a lot of other people were getting this procedure done today—if they could get through it, so could I, right? I filled out the pre-procedure questionnaire and checked "no" on most of the boxes. There was one that said, "Have you or a family member ever had cancer?" I checked "yes," with an explanation that my cousin battled breast cancer a few years back. I had a moment where I thought, "What if?" but quickly dismissed it, convincing myself that it wasn't cancer. I couldn't worry about all the what-ifs right now anyway. I had to concentrate on the here and now and get through this procedure. After a few moments passed, the nurse told me they were ready for me and wheeled me into the procedure room.

I was quickly put at ease as I saw a team of women and a lot of shiny brand-new equipment. They greeted me with smiles and told me what to expect. They said that it was a routine procedure and that the entire thing should take about forty-five minutes. For me, the scariest thing about the procedure was going under sedation, but the doctor soon put me at ease. The last thing I remember was counting down from ten, saying the number seven and then I was out.

The next thing I knew, I woke up in the recovery room and everything was a haze. I heard other people being wheeled out of their procedure rooms because only a thin curtain separated the patients in the recovery area. I lay there for a few minutes, trying to catch some rest and feel relief that the procedure was over. I heard the nurse tell the person to my right that she could get dressed and meet her ride outside in the main waiting room. Once she was gone, another patient was wheeled into her place, then the nurse went to the person on my left and told her to get dressed and meet her ride in the waiting room. A few more minutes passed, and I was starting to think did they forget me, but then the nurse came into my room and asked how I was doing, and I replied, "Doing good, just a little tired, but can I start getting dressed too and meet my ride outside?"

She smiled and asked if my ride was here. I told her that Cisco had been in the main waiting room the entire time, waiting until my procedure was over, and she told me that she would bring him in because the doctor wanted to talk to us. I remember closing my eyes thinking that this could not be good. What could she possibly say? What could possibly be wrong with me?

Cisco entered through the thin curtains, smiled, and sat down next to me while I was still lying on the gurney, feeling the effects of the sedation. I felt so helpless, but then he took my hand and asked me how it went. I told him how loopy I still felt, but overall, I felt good—and better with him there. We had only a few moments before the doctor walked in, so I wasn't able to tell him my concerns about the other patients being able to leave and the doctor wanting to speak to us. The doctor came in, stood next to me, and put her hand on my leg and said very sympathetically, "I wanted to talk to you both because I believe you have cancer."

It felt like the silence lasted forever. Then I felt Cisco's grip on my hand as if to wake me from this nightmare. Once the doctor had uttered the word "cancer," all the grogginess was sucked out of my body, I became attentive and immediately wanted to know more. I was the first to respond, "Wait, what do you mean? Did you say cancer? How do you know already?"

In a state of panic and concern, I think I asked those three questions in about two seconds flat. She explained to me that she has done a lot of these procedures and can tell by now if there are signs of cancer but that there would have to be more lab tests, along with a referral to a colorectal surgeon.

To say the least, all this information was overwhelming for me. Cancer? More tests? A colorectal surgeon? The only thing I understood was the word *cancer*, and nothing good ever comes from that word. I asked her, "So there is a chance that it isn't cancer, right?"

She responded with, "Yes, there is always that chance." That chance was what I was holding on to, but the look in her eyes prepared me to expect otherwise.

The drive home from the hospital was only fifteen minutes, but it seemed like an eternity. We sat in the car in silence for most of the ride, trying to grasp the information that had just been handed to us. I was still in shock, and Cisco finally broke the silence and said, "We have to look on the bright side. We can't fear what we don't know!" This was something I so wanted to believe. After all, there was a chance that it was not cancer, right?

Once at home, I called my immediate family to let them know what the gastroenterologist had told me. Hastily, I said, "Hi, Mom, so I just came back from my colonoscopy, and the doctor wants to do a few more tests because she thinks it may be cancerous."

I didn't want to worry my parents, so I tried to mask the news by speaking fast and hoping she didn't catch the word "cancerous," but once the word has been introduced into a conversation, there is no downplaying any scenario that the word brings.

She replied very nervously and loudly, "*What?* Did you say cancer? Val, are they sure?"

Then I heard her call my dad over to the phone so that he could listen to our conversation.

"No, Mom, they aren't sure yet. That's why they want to do more tests. There is a chance that it isn't cancer," I tried to say it in a matter-of-fact tone, with confidence to disguise my own worry and uneasiness, but I am sure my voice cracked a few times, and I am also sure that she caught that.

After a few moments of silence, she said in a sobbing voice, "OK, try to go get those other tests done as soon as you can, and I will continue to pray for you," and she handed the phone to my dad who said to me in a concerned voice, "Val, call me if you need anything."

I couldn't hold it in any longer, and I started to cry as I said, "Thanks, Dad. Tell Mom not to worry, and I'll call you as soon as I complete my tests. I love you both," and hung up the phone.

I know they were sick with worry and in shock as I have always been healthy. I continued to hope that the other tests would bring different news.

The next day I received a call from the colorectal surgeon, letting me know that I needed to get a colectomy procedure done as soon as possible to biopsy a part of my colon that she had concerns about. A colectomy procedure is the removal of a section of the large intestine (colon). The operation is done to treat colon cancer and other diseases that affect the colon. She explained that I was going to have a laparoscopic colectomy, in which an incision is made in my abdomen and the section of the diseased colon is removed. She pointed out that after the surgery, I would stay in the hospital until I regained bowel function, which may take a couple of days to a week, and that I would not be able to eat solid foods for three to four days after that. She also informed me that I had lost a lot of blood when I had been cramping and in pain. She said it could be dangerous to undergo sedation with such a low hemoglobin count, and she strongly recommended that I get a blood transfusion, which was scheduled for the following day.

I sat in the lab for four hours getting a blood transfusion and realized that I must have lost a lot of blood before my colonoscopy because I felt so much better and less lethargic afterward. I felt stronger and physically prepared for the surgery, but mentally and emotionally, I was a mess. There was a lot of preparation information that I received from my doctor and the surgeon regarding the colectomy, and it felt like everything was moving pretty fast. I really didn't have time to dwell on any possible bad news that I might receive. I just had to keep on going. My focus was on the next procedure.

The day of the colectomy was pretty somber and scary, as I knew I would be going under sedation again and the recovery time would be much longer. However, I didn't yet fully understand how physically hard it would be. When Cisco drove me to the hospital that morning, I was so relieved to see my mom, dad, Jett, and Sam at the hospital, cheering me on and letting me know that they would be right there waiting for me when I was finished with surgery. They were in the waiting room for the entire six hours, anticipating the results. As I went under sedation again, my last thought was that I couldn't wait to be done with this and see their smiling faces and have them stop worrying about me.

Waking up from surgery was terrifying at first, as I was disoriented to where I was and why I was there, and I didn't recognize anyone in the recovery room. There were a few other patients in the room recovering from their procedure, but this time there were no thin curtains to separate us. We were out in the open to see one another's vulnerabilities. I remember, as I woke up, the nurse told me to just lie there and she would bring one visitor in to see me. Then as I started to come out of the haze and remembered that I was at the hospital for a colectomy surgery, it became nerve-wracking because I wanted to know how everything went. *Here we go again*, I thought to myself. Why is she bringing in someone to see me? Did something go wrong again? Cisco walked into the recovery room and told me that the doctor had come to the waiting room to speak to my family and tell them that the surgery had gone really well. She was able to take out about seven centimeters of my colon and to have biopsied, along with the forty-seven lymph nodes she had also removed. The doctor told my family that I would receive a call within five days with the results of the biopsy, but for the next three days, I would be at the hospital recovering from the surgery. It was a lot of information for me to take in upon just waking up, but because I heard him say that the surgery went well, I was able to relax. I closed my eyes again for what I thought was only a few minutes.

I woke up in my own hospital room surrounded by family. My mom had made me a flower arrangement—one of her favorite creative hobbies—and Sam had given me a framed picture of Jett and me that she had placed by my bedside. It felt so good to see my family after surgery, and I drew on that moment for strength in the days that followed.

Recovery was pretty tough. I was forced to try to walk within hours of the surgery as they said it would speed up the healing process. It took all my effort to get out of bed and walk just a few feet, but Cisco knew I loved a challenge, so he would challenge me to walk ten extra feet every two hours. I seriously thought about giving up on that challenge, as the pain of walking was unbearable. To add to my misery, I could not eat solid foods for a week. Not being able to walk and not being able to eat anything was just debilitating for me. It was the first time in my life that I felt helpless.

The three days in the hospital were pretty long, but with Cisco's challenge of walking ten extra feet every time I got up, I was getting stronger. Soon enough, I was cruising slowly around the entire hospital wing. The doctors said that I was healing nicely and allowed me to go home after three days. This meant I still had two more long days until my biopsy results came in. While waiting for the results, I kept busy by continuing my walking to heal from the surgery, getting more rest and experimenting with new broths, as that was the only thing I could eat.

CHAPTER 4

The next few days were spent in my living room, as I still didn't have the strength to tackle going up and down the stairs, and the pain from surgery was still throbbing in my abdomen. I planted myself on the couch for those days and concentrated on healing and getting stronger. I kept hoping that the seven centimeters they took from my colon were the worst of it and that they had removed all of the cancerous tissue. I could not wait to receive the call, as anticipation and frustration were getting the best of me.

I finally received the call from my doctor right after the Fourth of July weekend while I was alone at home. The doctor told me calmly and compassionately that the biopsy results came back positive for stage 3A colon cancer and that an oncologist would give me a call tomorrow. *Colon cancer?! Stage 3A? How can this be?!* I thought to myself. I had so many questions for her, but the news was so paralyzing that all I could do was cry—words couldn't find their way out of my mouth. She told me that the oncologists would be able to answer my questions and that I could expect a call the following day.

After I hung up the phone, I took a few minutes to pull myself together and searched for the words I would use to let my mom and dad know. I called them. No answer. I called my Cisco. No answer. I called Sam. No answer. So I sat there crying in my bedroom for a few minutes as realization sunk in—life, as I knew it, was going to change.

Thoughts rushed through my mind.

I have a son who just started high school. I need to be there for his life's events, like his high school and college graduations. I want to see him get married one day, and I want to be able to meet my grandkids. We were just getting ready to have him go into driver's education to get his license.

I just met my boyfriend six months ago, and he just helped me through this whole surgery thing. Now I have to tell him I have cancer—not something you can expect a person to tackle early on in a relationship.

My best friend and I still have two more continents to visit, including our planned South America trip in four months. Not to mention, we have seen each other through the best and worst of times, now I have to tell her I have this disease.

As far as my mom and dad, I didn't want them to worry about me and see me go through more tough times. So I sat there, anticipating their reactions and how I could comfort them. I had to somehow reassure them that I will beat this—I was trying to reassure myself at the same time. In the midst of this storm, I wondered how to adjust my sails.

I saw my mom's name pop up on my cell phone. I quickly pulled myself together and told her that the doctor called me back, and I told her that my test results came back positive for stage 3A colon cancer. Even saying it to her made me tear up again. There was a long pause, then I heard her start to cry, softly at first, then uncontrollably as she dropped the phone. My dad picked up the phone, and I told him the news I had been given. Silence, once again, came over the phone, and he hurriedly said they would be right over.

The conversation went the same with Sam and Cisco and then again when Jett came home from school. That night they all came over to my house, including my brother, Brandon, and my sister-in-law, Shana, to let me know that I could get through this and that if I needed any help, they would be there for me as they always have been. That night I found the strength to walk up the stairs to sleep in the comfort of my own bed for the first time in a week. The pain in my abdomen was secondary to the pain I was feeling mentally and emotionally.

The next day, still weak from the surgery and anxiously awaiting my oncologist's call, what did I do to pass the time? I jumped on the Internet, not for self-diagnosis this time, but to get more information on colon cancer. Another tip: Don't do this either! The worst-case scenarios always pop up first, but I was able to find some good information about colon cancer from reliable websites like the American Cancer Society and the Mayo Clinic.

I learned that colon cancer is the third most-commonly diagnosed cancer and the second leading cause of cancer death in men and women combined in the United States— every 9.3 minutes, a person in the United States dies of colon cancer. While rates for colon cancer in adults fifty and older have been declining, incidence rates in adults younger than 50 have been increasing. That was more than enough for me to handle, particularly the bit about someone dying every 9.3 seconds. I closed my computer and just waited for the doctor to call.

She gave me a call in the late morning and told me she had an opening for an appointment that afternoon, so I jumped on it and told her I would be right over. I still needed help getting around because of my surgery, and fortunately, Cisco and Sam were more than happy to take me and provide emotional support—which, at this point, I thought I didn't need. My parents also offered to come, but I didn't want to worry them any more than I already had, so I told them I would update them once we get more information.

So what exactly is stage 3A colon cancer? It means that the tumors are within the colon walls and also involve some of my lymph nodes. The doctor took out seven centimeters of my colon and forty-seven lymph nodes. Of the forty-seven lymph nodes, forty-six of them came back all clear. It was the forty-seventh one that tested positive for cancer. Damn that forty-seventh one!

Once in the doctor's office, there were a few treatment options offered, from a less aggressive chemotherapy approach to a very aggressive regimen. The information was given in a very fair and balanced way so that I could weigh all my options. Of course, I asked her what she would recommend, and she stated that since I was still young, strong, and healthy (even though I really didn't feel that in that moment, being fresh out of surgery and diagnosed with stage 3A colon cancer), she recommended the very aggressive chemotherapy regimen. Because of the forty-seventh lymph node coming back cancerous, I wanted to make sure my body was completely rid of cancer. Cis and Sam agreed that I could handle the aggressive route, but then I had to make another decision, about which aggressive regimen I wanted to go with. She described the two available approaches, and I noticed that one of the chemotherapy drugs was manufactured by the biotech company where I worked. Bingo! That seemed like a sign that it was the regimen I needed to be on, and that decision was easily made.

My regimen included taking two tablets of chemotherapy a day and an infusion, which would be scheduled once a week for three to four hours each week. My oncologist said that I would have eight cycles of two weeks for six months. So that basically means that after every two weeks of intensive chemo, I had a one-week break to let my body recover before the next cycle started. I wanted to start right away and be done with it, but because of my colectomy surgery, my oncologist recommended that I wait four weeks before I started chemotherapy. I could barely walk and was now facing down this aggressive chemotherapy regimen, so I had to heal first.

As someone dealing with something so life-altering, I had a lot on my mind. Now that I knew what I had to deal with and everything I was up against, I had to ask myself how was I going to present it to the outside world? I had been off work for about two weeks at this point, and my coworkers were starting to inquire why I was out sick for so long. My good friends, especially the ones who were planning our next trip, were asking why I hadn't returned their e-mails and calls.

How would I tell people I had been diagnosed with cancer? Was I really up for all the questions they would ask me? It was the day my world came crashing down, but it was also the day I realized the importance of the work that my company does for cancer patients and the humanity that goes hand in hand with our line of work.

Everything happens for a reason, and on this day, things came full circle. I thought back to my earlier years and how I longed for a more purposeful and fulfilling career, and then I met Ingrid, who nudged me to apply for a position at the company. I thought about how important that decision was and how I had found that purpose with my current company, which help develop drugs for cancer patients. Now I was going to be on the receiving end of those drugs we develop.

I took it day by day. Once I found out about my plans for the next six months, I contacted my manager, Christine, and let her know what was going on with me. We talked for a while, even though she was at work—that really meant a lot to me, as I knew how busy she was. She asked me what I was doing that night, and I told her that we were just going to a little restaurant for my first official meal out in about three weeks. You can guess what happened next—she showed up at the restaurant! My eyes lit up to see her, she gave me a really great hug, and I just cried in her arms. During dinner, she asked me what she should tell our colleagues at work. Out of concern, they had been inquiring about my absence for the last two weeks. This is the moment I realized that I had to own my journey. I told her to let them know my diagnosis and that I would be OK. She reminded me of all the contacts I had made at work and mentioned that I should reach out to them to find out more about the regimen I was about to embark on.

That's the first time I said "I will be OK" with a little hesitation, and I knew I had to come to terms with it. For me, being OK meant putting faith in the drugs we developed as a company. The hesitation came from uncertainty over how my body would react to it. Would I be physically and mentally strong enough to endure six months of chemo? Being OK also meant I had tons of support from my family. The hesitation there was over the fact that I'm not one to burden people with my own problems or to have them worry about me.

Once the word was out at work, there was an outpouring of encouragement from the colleagues I had connected with during my many years at the company. These people helped reassure me that I was getting the best care and latest treatments available and that the drug my company manufactures would add years to my prognosis.

Owning my journey also included letting my friends know. Again, I had to ask myself, was I ready for that? I had always had an active lifestyle, surrounded by friends and family, and I was known for my positive energy and joie de vivre. I loved entertaining and had friends over frequently on the weekend—would they look at me differently now?

Once people find out you have cancer, the conversations seem to always turn somber. I could always have those somber conversations with myself, but I couldn't let those pity parties run my life, so I didn't entertain those thoughts often. This was just a tough chapter of my life that I needed to get through, and I was looking to do so much more after I beat this disease. Trust me, I understood the severity of it, and sometimes I just needed an escape to see and experience life beyond this terrible disease.

I guess this is why the term *cancer survivor* bothers me. The word *survivor* is typically used to signify a person remaining alive after an event in which others have died. Yes, we have lost people in battle caused by this ugly disease but by no means because they wanted to die. They fought just as hard. Cancer patients are all faced with the same struggle—to survive! It saddens me deeply when I hear someone has passed away from cancer, as I know how hard that struggle is and how much they too wanted to be called a cancer survivor. By no fault of their own was it something that they chose to endure—no one is immune from cancer. There also may have been some healthcare gaps, or perhaps they just didn't have access to care. It's what life dealt them, and in the end, the ultimate goal is to beat this disease, and sadly, some do not. This is why I prefer to be called a *cancer warrior,* as all who have battled this disease are warriors. Bravery and courage are two important qualities for a warrior to have, and more importantly, this term is inclusive to everyone who has fought this disease, whether they have lost their battle or just started to fight—plus, "cancer warrior" sounds pretty badass!

One of the mottos I like to live by, and that I tell Jett often, is "When you can't control what's happening, challenge yourself to control the way you respond to what's happening. That's where your power is." And there were a lot of things out of my control around my diagnosis! I had to look inward to find the strength to control the way I responded to things. It wasn't easy, but that's what family and friends are for—to help you through life when things aren't easy.

Of course, I told my closest friends first, which included my travel friends. We decided to call ourselves "The Quest for 7 Crew," meaning the seven continents. We had started using the hashtag, #Questfor7Crew in some of our Instagram posts from our earlier travels, then it sort of stuck and became our nickname. They were just as shocked as I was to learn about my diagnosis—we had just come back from South Africa eight months ago. They asked me how I was feeling, and since I had just been diagnosed, and still a bit numb from the news, I told them, "Remember that time in South Africa when we were on safari and being charged by that elephant and our Jeep was stuck in a ditch? It feels somewhat like that—right now, I'm stuck in the ditch, facing the charge." They appreciated the comparison as they knew exactly what that feeling was like, but they also knew that it was my way of downplaying it. With that, they lent me their full support, and I wouldn't have expected less from them. They also reminded me that we eventually got out of the ditch, it wasn't easy, but eventually, we got out of it. I can always count on them to lift my spirits with memories of our travels and the endless laughs we have had throughout the years. I knew that I wasn't going to make the trip to South America that we had planned for that year because of my treatments, so I told them I would be there in spirit and to take a lot of photos for me. I had a different journey planned out for me that year.

One of the first people I told was my friend Lisa, who also worked at the biotech company, and was one of the first people I had met at work ten-plus years ago. She too was a single mom, raising twins just a little older than Jett. I would always look to her for advice as I know she would have some strong suggestions for tough situations—and we would always end up laughing. Lisa works in the biooncology department at our company, and among the connections she had made with people over her tenure were a great many doctors with whom I was then able to connect and discuss my diagnosis and treatment plan. I took full advantage of that free education and the advice given by those doctors. I was able to ask them whether they agreed that the aggressive treatment I was about to embark on was something I could handle, and they gave it their approval. I was lucky to have that access to scientists with their knowledge and was once again feeling grateful for what our company does to help people diagnosed with cancer.

My quest for the seven continents had taken a detour into a quest for more knowledge and education about colon cancer and how I could eventually beat this incurable disease. I have only great things to say about the hospital where I received treatment, Kaiser Permanente. From the time I started feeling pain, through my surgery, to my pending chemotherapy treatments, I had been informed and advised every step of the way. It gave me great comfort, knowing that they had my full medical records and didn't have to wait to get access to other medical records that different doctors may have. They would schedule me for educational consultations to let me know what was to happen every step of the way, and I was able to bring my family and friends with me so if they had any questions, they could ask. I had pre-surgery and post-surgery consultations for my colectomy, as well as a pre-chemotherapy appointment, to know more about the process. If ever I wasn't feeling well enough to make it out to an appointment, they would send a nurse over to do the education and answer any questions that me or my family might have in the comfort of my home. I was also lucky enough to have what is known as a patient navigator, who I could call if I ever had any questions throughout my treatments. I was well-informed at every stage of my treatment.

As far as informing my wider network of friends, I was always active on social media with my traveling excursions. I had to ask myself, would I continue to stay active about this chapter in my life? Then I remembered that I had told myself that I was going to own this journey. I would face it head on. In the past, when I had posted about my trips, people would reach out to give me tips on the city that I was traveling to, and I found their insights very helpful. I was hoping that this journey would not be any different, and with that in mind, I took the first step and posted about my diagnosis.

I had many people reach out with messages of support and to let me know of either their own personal journey (sometimes ones they weren't comfortable being public about) or a loved one's journey and how they dealt with the situation. It was therapeutic for me to know what others have done to get through their treatments and to gain insights ahead of my first day of chemotherapy as well as the months that would follow. I gained strength from this first- and secondhand knowledge that you could not get from a textbook. I thanked them for their wisdom, and they expressed gratitude for me being so open about my journey and told me that they looked forward to my future posts, that they might provide strength for people going through their own personal struggles. The pressure was now on, stupid cancer had better watch out!

Even with all the reliable information I had received from the Internet and all my doctors, I do also have to call out the bad information that I received. I learned quickly that everyone's journey is not the same. I would hear about adverse events that would happen to people on their cancer journey, and I had to compartmentalize this information. But I would also hear all the good things chemotherapy did for people who were now living happily in remission. The good information outweighed the bad.

I would also get spam e-mails from unknown people telling me to take this "magic pill" and I would be cured of cancer—or any disease—by a certain time frame. These types of communications would really upset me, as I am a firm believer in science—working in biotech for over a decade tends to do that to you. I knew how much work it takes for a drug to get to market, and for these companies to promote a "magic pill" plays on the already-fragile emotions of the sick with something that is just not scientifically proven. It's just bad education that promotes false hopes. I put my full trust in science. After all, I viewed misinformation as another disease that I did not want to catch.

Don't get me wrong, I do believe that alternative and traditional medicine *can* coexist. For example, when I was discussing the potential side effects that come with chemotherapy and my overall mental health about having this disease, I brought the subject of cannabinoids for cancer patients up to my doctor. I had heard that it helps overcome the often-debilitating side effects of cancer and its treatment. As always, she took a fair and balanced approach, which is something I always appreciated about her and gave the good and bad of taking marijuana. Back then, it still wasn't legal in California, so she wrote me a medical marijuana prescription that then I filled at a dispensary in Oakland. As things became tougher during my treatments, I decided to try it, and it did help me deal with the pain. Did it cure me? Nope, but it helped! It coexisted with chemotherapy, supplementing my treatments.

So there I was, the night before my first infusion, armed with the correct information backed by science and having successfully compartmentalized the bad information. My treatment plan had been given the endorsement of my trusted colleagues, and with the love of family and friends supporting me, cancer didn't stand a chance! And it certainly didn't have the power to control my life. Though I slept fitfully, I went to bed early that night, as I knew I would need all the strength I had to fight this ugly disease. After all, we were going eight rounds for six months. With too much at stake, there was no way I was going to throw in the towel! Let round one begin— *ding ding!*

CHAPTER 5

All the preparations leading up to treatment meant that the actual first day of my intravenous (IV) chemotherapy treatment crept up on me. It was here before I knew what was happening, and I found myself thinking *sh*! just got real!* I felt physically prepared for it as I was recovered from surgery and was able to do normal things on my own again. Mentally, I was scared but ready to rid my body of this disease. The night before the IV, I took two tablets of the chemotherapy drug my company manufactures and felt OK the next morning. I thought I felt a little nauseous, but reflecting now, it was most likely nerves, as I was more worried about the three-to four-hour intravenous treatment.

The preparation instructions for the infusion said to wear comfy clothes and bring something to keep me busy to pass the time since I would be there for a few hours. I thought I would put on some makeup to make me feel better, lift my mood for the day, and most importantly, show cancer that I was ready to beat this. Somewhat similar to how Native Americans decorated the face and body before battle, it was my war paint. As far as keeping busy, Sam and Cisco were there to help me through my first infusion day, and they kept me busy with stories that kept my mood up.

As I walked into the infusion room and waited for a nurse to help me, there was a group of elderly ladies who looked at me up and down and politely but firmly said, "This area is for cancer patients only. If you are picking someone up, go to the other end of the check-in counter." My eyes started welling up with tears as I found myself wanting to be accepted and comforted in a world I had never even wanted to be part of. I took a deep breath, smiled, sat down beside them, and said, "I am a cancer patient."

Just hearing myself say "I am a cancer patient" was another step in owning my journey. It felt and sounded so strange. The ladies were overcome with silence. Then you could see the understanding come over the group, and they smiled and broke the silence by welcoming me into this unknown territory by telling me about their diagnoses and how long each had been in treatment. They even rushed around the infusion room to find a nurse to help me. It was like being in an exclusive club that no one wants to be a part of, but only members can truly understand. The conversation turned somber, as they couldn't believe someone so young was diagnosed with colon cancer and undergoing chemotherapy. They said, "Young lady, you have the strength to do this, so go fight as hard as you can!"

Again, my eyes started to well up with tears and said, "Oh, I will!" and I wished them well on their journeys.

As I was escorted to the infusion chair, my first impression of the chair was pretty ominous, and I hated it. I felt like a dead woman walking as I digested the fact that I would have to be in this chair for four hours receiving chemotherapy. I found myself thinking, *This is going to be a long four hours*, and I realized that I had to rethink this. I quickly came to the realization that it wasn't the chair that I hated, but it was cancer that was the cause of my hate. I had to pivot—fast—to turn this into a positive situation, so I told myself that this was just a chair that would provide comfort for me for the next three to four hours during my IV cocktail, so I shouldn't be afraid of it or hate it. I convinced myself that it was one of those Brookstone recliners, the big leather ones that massaged you and you were able to elevate your feet and recline. While the chair and I were getting acquainted, I realized that it actually was very comfy. The nurse was busy getting the IV bags ready, which was even scarier, but again, having worked for a biotech company for many years, I believed in the science and the ten-plus years of development that it had taken for this drug to get to market. I truly believed this drug would help save my life.

And then it was time to get infused. I sat there nervous as hell, and the nurse sensed it, so she gave me a smile and whispered, "See those two older ladies over there? If they can handle it, you surely can!"

I smiled at her and said jokingly, "But they are so much more feisty than me!"

We laughed, and she said not to worry as the first infusion she was going to give me was a medication to avert side effects or hypersensitivity reactions—in other words, an antihistamine. By this time, I was used to being poked and prodded, so the IV didn't bother me. I was also too preoccupied with the side effects of what chemo would do to me after the infusion.

I had been told, before my treatments, that the various side effects might include fatigue, hair loss, mouth sores, nausea, vomiting, nerve damage, diarrhea, bruising, and infection. The uncertainty factor of which of these side effects I might experience was very worrisome and something I couldn't prepare for. After the twenty-minute antihistamine infusion—which went pretty quickly and I hardly felt any discomfort other than in my mind—it was time to get infused with the chemo drug.

They allowed me a ten-minute break to wrap my head around what was about to happen and asked me if I had any questions that they could help answer. I was pretty confident about the process, so I didn't have any questions. It was a quick change of the needle, and then before I knew it, the chemotherapy drug was being administered into my body. I felt a different rush into my system than I had with the antihistamine drug, and I took a deep breath and prayed, *Please, God, let this work.* The kind nurse smiled at me and said, "Look, you are doing it!" It gave me a sense of empowerment over this awful disease—yep, I *am* doing it and will do everything in my power to beat this disease. Cisco and Sam kept me pretty busy with conversations and laughter for the entire four hours.

My mom and dad also stopped by, even though I had asked them not to, but I know it was so hard for them to deal with me being sick. I had asked them not to come because I didn't know how I was going to handle my first infusion and I didn't want to continue to worry them. I totally understood why they wanted to see me—after all, they were my strong-willed parents. I was so happy to see them, and I could tell that it eased all our anxieties for them to be there. I had to show them how strong I was—I didn't want them to worry anymore. My mom, being a true Filipina, expressed a lot of her love and care for me (and others) by cooking. For this first day of my treatment, she had made me some soup to keep my strength up. She continued to make me soup every week that I had my infusions, which I found comforting. Nothing is better than having your mom's food when going through such adversity.

After my first infusion, we all gathered at my home—my parents, Brandon, Shana, Jett, Sam, and Cisco. I love entertaining and having family over, so I would typically be running around the kitchen making sure everyone had their plates and cups filled, but this time felt very different. I couldn't do any of that. I was tired—like, *really* tired! But I felt great comfort from having them all there with me. I sat on the couch and recounted with them how it went and reassured them that it was something I could handle. I soon fell asleep for what felt like only a nap but ended up being four hours of deep sleep.

For the next two weeks, I took a chemotherapy pill twice a day. To overcome any mental hurdles, I would tell myself it was just vitamins. By the end of the two weeks, I was exhausted but had no real side effects other than feeling very lethargic. I was feeling like maybe I was going to get away with something! If only the side effects had stayed mild for me . . .

After each of the eight chemo cycles, I began to feel different side effects with a lot more intensity, and my blood work started to reflect that. My white blood cells would fluctuate along with the rest of my labs. By the second cycle, I was still feeling OK, no nausea or vomiting, but I felt a little more tired after every pill I took. As a goal, I kept my eye on that third week of each cycle, when I was free from the chemo treatments and infusions and could let my body recover. And not only did those weeks off help me physically, but they also helped me mentally. I was able to feel free of the chemo medications and able to take a glimpse back into the kingdom of the well. During my off weeks, I was able to reconnect with friends and have them over for lunch or dinner and share some laughs. I wasn't bound by taking medications at a certain time. By the end of my off cycle, I had regained the strength to do it all over again. As you would expect, I was over it after the first cycle, but cancer wasn't, so I had to muster up every ounce of courage in me to do it all over again for at least seven more rounds.

By the grace of God, I was still doing OK after the third cycle. We had just celebrated Jett's fifteenth birthday at my mom and dad's house, where she made a huge spread of food for all of us to enjoy. Fortunately, I didn't experience any nausea or vomiting as a side effect. I had been really worried about that, as I'd heard horror stories about it coming on from out of nowhere and at the worst times. And although my appetite was diminished because of the medications, I was happy to be able to celebrate my son's birthday and eat at least a little bit of my favorite Filipino foods that my mom had prepared. It was a great day, and cancer didn't get to take it away!

Shortly after my third cycle, Cisco was asked by his company to attend a training in the Midwest for a week, and it happened to fall during my off week for treatments. During my post-third-cycle appointment with my oncologist, Cisco surprised me by asking my doctor if it would be OK for me to travel domestically. International trips were definitely out of the question, per the doctor, and I didn't want to take a chance to be away from unfamiliar healthcare in case something was to happen, but I hadn't thought about domestic travel. She took a look at my latest lab results and said everything looked fine, my white blood cell count seemed to be holding, and she gave me the OK to travel domestically. If I couldn't continue my quest for the seven continents, I might as well start a new quest for the fifty states! It had been so long since I had traveled anywhere other than the infusion room. I needed this break from my scheduled routine of doctors' appointments and was looking forward to just getting away and doing normal things.

Two days later, I packed my bags and jumped on a plane to meet Cisco in Omaha, Nebraska. It was my first time in that state, and the excitement of jumping on an airplane to visit a new place and set my eyes on new sights was exhilarating. After his training, we rented a car and traveled through Nebraska, Iowa, and South Dakota. Cisco is an avid motorcycle enthusiast, so he was excited to see Sturgis, South Dakota, where the Sturgis Motorcycle Rally is held annually. I was excited to see anything other than the infusion room; however, my favorite part of the trip was seeing Mount Rushmore National Memorial in all its glory. It was just as grand and epic as I'd thought it would be.

It was a beautiful autumn trip to the Midwest, seeing the leaves in their striking fall colors fall gently to the ground. I was reminded that those leaves will be back again in the spring with new growth, as no winter lasts forever. The season was changing for me as well. This trip was exactly what I needed to feel renewed, regenerated, and normal. I was ready to tackle the second half of my treatments.

After less than a week, I was back in the Bay Area and ready to face cycle four. If the second half was to be like the first, then I felt prepared, but this was wishful thinking on my part once again. A new side effect seemed to appear at every cycle from here on out. With cycle four in late September, I started to feel two of the worst side effects: cold sensitivity and a metallic taste in my mouth. While eating cold foods like a salad or even drinking cold water with ice, it felt like shards of glass were going down my throat—to say it was painful is an understatement. My mom's soups were a lifesaver. Somehow moms always know best. The cold sensitivity wasn't just limited to food, but my whole body also felt cold to a point where I was always wearing a heavy sweater or jacket. Mind you, it was late September in the San Francisco Bay Area, and that's when we have our "summer weather."

The metallic taste was another sensitivity I experienced. After finishing my meals, I would have this weird taste in my mouth. I've come to understand that it's a taste disorder medically known as dysgeusia. It is an abnormal or impaired sense of taste or an unpleasant alteration of taste sensation. When I would eat, I would feel this persistent metallic, sour, bitter, bad taste in the mouth. It was heightened by drinking out of metal glasses and using silver utensils to eat. It was such an awful and uncomfortable feeling. As if things couldn't get any crazier, when we would eat at restaurants, I felt insane ordering soup and hot water and asking for plastic utensils during our Indian summer while wearing winter outfits because I was always cold.

During cycle five, another side effect decided to surface: I would start to bruise and bleed easily. So not only was I tired and weak and everything I ate tasted awful, but to add to that, I looked like I was battered and beat-up. I would have bruises just from having my watch on, and any pressure on my skin for more than a few minutes would leave a black-and-blue mark. A small cut would take a while to scab to stop bleeding. I remember one time when I cut myself while slicing onions, it was a small superficial cut but took about an hour to stop bleeding while before my diagnosis, it would have taken no more than fifteen minutes. My doctors said this was brought about by my low platelets and that I should be extra careful to not cut myself or cause any bruises to myself. I looked and felt like a walking zombie! At this point, I was definitely feeling the effects of chemotherapy and could not wait until it was over. I just had to keep thinking positive—only three more cycles left.

Cycle six started in November and brought another horrible side effect, peripheral neuropathy, which was just as bad as it sounds. It's a result of damage to the nerves outside of the brain and spinal cord. It often causes weakness, numbness, and pain, usually in your hands and feet. It can also affect other areas of your body. Luckily, it only affected my hands and feet and only when it was cold, but we were in November, so I experienced this painful symptom often. I couldn't go outside without wearing gloves and at least two pairs of socks. If I didn't, my hands and feet would feel like they were being pricked by sharp needles. I had to buy some hand warmers to keep inside my jackets just to keep the pain at bay. Having this side effect made receiving treatments in the winter even more painful, and I had to make sure I was well bundled up for those treatment days.

Before each cycle, I would have to have a complete blood count (CBC) to check my blood levels, especially my white blood cell (WBC) and my platelets count. White blood cells fight off infection in the body, and platelets form clots to stop or prevent bleeding. Up until this point, my levels had been OK. There had been a concern about my platelets being low in cycle five, but they had stayed at a consistent number since then and didn't drop any further. As with the previous cycles, an introduction to a new side effect was almost expected, and cycle seven proved no different. This time, to everyone's surprise, it brought a pause to my treatments because my labs showed that my white blood cell count was very low and that it was a cause for concern. With a low white blood cell count and, in particular, a low level of neutrophils, I was at a higher risk of developing an infection. If an infection were to develop while my white blood cell count was low, my body couldn't protect itself. Such an infection could, in some severe cases, lead to death.

Treatment would have to be paused while this complication was dealt with. This was a huge blow to me as I only had two more cycles left, but my body was giving me signs that it needed rest. So before any more treatments were to continue, I would now have to get a shot in my hip to help boost my white blood cell count, in hopes that the count would be high enough to continue treatment for that week. The treatment I did was called white blood cell growth factors or colony-stimulating factors (CSFs). CSFs are drugs that help prevent infection during chemotherapy and increase the number of white cells in your blood.

After this small pause in cycle seven, allowing my body to rest and recover and with the help of the CSFs, I would be able to continue treatments. Now instead of ending my treatments in December, my last treatment would be scheduled for January. Although cycle seven started late, I was relieved to know that my body was receptive to the CSF drug and that my last cycle would be slated with no further delay.

It was finally here, my last infusion. I remember waking up early on December 28 and telling Cisco to hurry up and get ready. I was in such a rush to get this morning over with. It was a cold morning, but it was the first time I didn't mind putting on my gloves and two pairs of socks to keep warm because of my neuropathy. Jett was up early to wish me well on my last treatment, so we had a light breakfast together. We had just celebrated Christmas a few days before, and I was hoping I could cash in on my Christmas wishes that morning: for me to finally be done with this awful disease and for someone to find a cure for it so that no one else would have to go through these treatments.

As I walked into the infusion room for the last treatment, it felt very different from previous times. The nurses welcomed me, as they always did, but this time it was a welcome to never come back, which was well received by me. I remember nestling my body into that cozy chair that I loved to hate and closing my eyes. I woke up when the nurse started to pull the needle out of my arm, and she told me that I had been asleep for the entire four hours. I suppose I rested so well because I was confident that it would be my last time. I walked out of there full of hope, and we went home to celebrate with my family that the end was nearly in sight.

Chapter 6

By taking my last two pills, my entire chemotherapy regime was completed, and I was hoping for no other side effects and that my labs wouldn't show any more signs of trouble. All I could do at this point was wait to see if cancer was still present in my body. I had to bide my time until the end of the month for more labs and another CT scan to see if malignant tumors would show up. It was going to be a long three weeks until those tests were done, but it was a brand-new year, and I had high hopes that this year would bring much better news, new beginnings, and a lot more happy memories for me. I had to hold on to hope that things were going to turn around for the better. After all, I had big plans for 2016, and I wasn't going to let cancer stop them. While waiting until I could take my tests, I had some time on my hands to reflect on the past year and to let my body rest and recover.

It had been such a tough six and a half months. I couldn't believe I had completed eight cycles of chemo. It was the hardest thing I had ever done in my life. It consumed me physically, mentally, and spiritually. I guess the saying is true, "You never know how strong you are until being strong is your only choice."

Looking back at it, there were so many times I had wanted to give up—like at every cycle. I remember telling the nurse in the middle of one of my treatments to remove the IV and I'll come back tomorrow to finish my treatment session. It was the same thing I tried to tell the nurses when I was delivering Jett, all ten pounds of him. I think the chemo nurses found it funny that I would try to negotiate my way out of my treatments, but I was being serious. Some days I was just too exhausted, and not knowing what the results would be after chemo ended wasn't convincing enough to continue. Their answer would be a calming smile and a quick pep talk to let me know how well I was doing and that it wouldn't be too long before I finished my treatment for that week. I would tell myself, well, if they have faith in me to continue, I should put that same faith in myself. Plus, all my family and friends had that same faith. Who am I to let them down? It was that extra push I needed to keep on going and look past my current infusion treatment.

In the back of my mind, I would always think every cycle, what if this chemo thing doesn't work? And what if my body isn't strong enough to go more rounds? What would happen to Jett? He's still young, and he needs me, plus you only get one mom. I thought about my mom, dad, and brother and how I couldn't let them down. Cisco and I had just met, it couldn't end this soon—we still had way too much to experience together. And Sam and I still had lots of BFF things to do together, including traveling to those other continents. I had to learn to keep that damn "What if it doesn't work?" question at bay during those six months and replace it with "What will I do after it works?" It wasn't easy at first, but with the help of family and friends, it became easier. Because they saw my life beyond cancer, it helped me see it through their lens and visualize beating this disease.

While I had been on leave from work for those six months, concentrating on beating this disease, I knew I had to keep busy so it didn't consume me. Sam knew that I loved to keep my mind busy by learning new things, whether it was a new craft or a new skill. So right after my colectomy surgery, she proposed that we study for the California real estate exam and take the test and get our real estate licenses. I think she knew it would keep me off the Internet, reading all the fake health news on cancer, and saw it as a way to keep my mind off the treatments. Plus, it was a subject that interested both of us. I gave it a whole two seconds of thought before I answered, "Yes!" I've always been interested in real estate, especially after my parents owned the apartment building in Daly City. So in early July, we purchased our real estate books and took online classes together. I would bring my books to my chemotherapy appointments to take my mind off the treatments, and on days while Cisco was at work and Jett at school, I would read and study until one of them came home. It gave me a sense of normalcy and preparing for a future after I beat cancer. It gave me other things to think about other than chemotherapy and kept me sane and my mind busy as I learned the ins and outs of real estate. Sam and I discussed the chapters and lectures, and it was the perfect distraction from cancer, which I needed at that point in my journey.

Right after my cycle six treatment in November, we had enough credits to take the real estate exam and felt confident enough about the information we had learned. We waited until it was my chemo off week and then ventured to Oakland and took our test live at the state building. About thirty people were sitting individually in front of desktop computers ready to take the exam. We were all spaced out so that we would not be able to see one another's computer screens. It reminded me of being in school, which I liked—a familiar scary feeling once the exam started. Sam completed her test first and handed in her exam at the back of the room. I followed a few minutes later, and as I handed in my exam, they inserted it into a computer and I was given a folded receipt. The lady at the counter told me that the results were on the receipt that I had just received. I remember thinking, *Wow, I wish my chemo results came this fast*. Neither Sam nor I knew we were going to receive the results so soon. We thought they would mail us our results. I opened up the receipt before heading out the door where Sam was waiting. It simply said, "Passed."

After I walked out the door, we ran toward each other smiling and excitedly asking the same question, "How did you do?" We answered at the same time, "I passed!" We were now official California real estate agents. It was such a great feeling to accomplish something we worked so hard on during this unusual and trying time. For me, I felt normal again. We left the state building that day feeling accomplished and talked about how to put our real estate licenses to good use. It felt really good to make plans for the future.

I guess that's what I had missed the most during the prior six months: normalcy, including making plans for the future. Although my priorities in life had changed and beating this disease had become paramount, I still longed for the good old days when cancer didn't touch my life. I felt like I was overdosing on cancer information at every turn and I couldn't get away from it. People would ask me how I was doing, and I didn't know how to answer, so I would just tell them honestly that I was doing OK and trying to keep my spirits up. I wished I could tell them that the chemo was definitely working and that I would be just fine and back to normal after my treatments, but I just didn't know. I think they understood. It's an unspoken worry when you know someone who has been diagnosed with cancer and their future is uncertain. The answer to "How are you doing?" can never be wrong or judged.

Among the many surprises during my six-month journey were the gifts that my family, friends, and colleagues would send me when I was receiving treatments. Flowers sent to me uplifted my mood for the day, and inspirational books kept me smiling even during my treatments. I also received gift cards from restaurants and meal delivery services that really helped on those days when I just needed to stay in bed but needed to make something for dinner for Jett. All the gifts I received were very thoughtful, and I was very grateful to have such caring family members and friends.

There was one gift that I received that stood out. My friend Pattie gave me a nail salon gift card. I know it sounds weird, but this became a place I looked forward to going to during those six months while I was in treatment. It was my glimpse back into the kingdom of the well. You see, the ladies at the nail salon didn't know I had cancer. The conversations didn't center around me and my health or that stupid disease. It was a place I could escape to and have those lighthearted and sometimes belly-aching laughs. I felt normal again and able to connect with the outside world without being a cancer patient. It was a safe place for me, where I felt unbothered by cancer and all the uncertainty this disease brings. So once every two weeks, if I wasn't too tired from my treatments, I would gladly leave cancer at home, venture out to the nail salon, and just be a person getting her nails done. For an hour, I didn't have to think about that ugly disease, and for that moment, all was well as I straddled both kingdoms.

My mom and dad kept me pretty busy too. They would call me and ask how the cancer warrior was doing today and remind me that I should eat before I go into battle, and she made sure I did by making me soups to keep my strength up. My mom didn't like me being alone during the daytime, so she would call me, and we would go shopping and walk around the mall. She would call it her exercise, and I would joke with her and tell her the only things we were exercising were our wallets. We all grew closer during this time; my mom and dad would come over on the weekends more often, and they and our close friends would watch football and basketball games with us to keep things normal for me.

Still, my international trips with my friends were something I really missed. My doctor did give me the green light to travel domestically, and when my labs looked good and I felt strong enough, I took advantage. It became apparent that a break from my everyday routine of doctor appointments, infusion rooms, and medications was an important part of my healing process.

In November of that year, I had another opportunity to travel and take a break from my routine. Jett and I tagged along with Cisco and his family on a road trip to Los Angeles and spent the weekend at Disneyland. I couldn't think of a better place to be than "The Happiest Place on Earth" during my off-chemo cycle, and it felt good to be in the Southern California sun as I was still suffering from peripheral neuropathy. Feeling the sun on my skin as we walked around made the neuropathy almost disappear. The laughter of family as we made new memories was priceless, and the exhilarating rides created an excitement that I haven't felt in a while. It was exactly what I needed to feel renewed and rejuvenated. Even though it wasn't a big international trip, it allowed me to pause, slow down, and appreciate any trip I was allowed to go on.

As I reflected, it also put all those pre-cancer trips in a brand-new light, and I appreciated and treasured those moments and places I have visited so much more. A sense of gratitude and appreciation overcame me for all the places that I had already visited, and I looked forward to recovering so I could continue making new memories and experience new places.

Before I knew it, it was the night before my blood draw and CT scan to see if any sign of cancer was still present. Anticipation got the best of me, and I was up all night. So many emotions raced through me. I was excited, scared, anxious, and nervous all at the same time. Everything I had done, from my first CT scan to my last chemo pill, was about to come to a head with these results. I remembered something

Sam once told me, "The body achieves what the mind believes." I had to get a grip on those emotions once again and keep thinking positive. I had learned to embrace the struggle as I knew it wasn't going to last forever. I had retrained my mind to believe that I could beat this so that my body would follow.

In no time, the morning was upon us, and Cis and I woke up early—I don't think either of us had slept well that night. The lab opened up at 7:00 a.m., but we were the first ones there at 6:30 a.m. They took what felt like pints of blood from me, but it really was just five big vials of blood. Besides, being poked and prodded at didn't bother me anymore, as I had to get my blood drawn every two weeks. The only thing different this time was that they took an extra vial of blood. Our next stop at the hospital was the radiology department, where I had an appointment for my CT scan. They would have to inject that awful iodine IV into me again, but this time I didn't mind as I was anxious for the results. I lay on the bed and thought back to my first CT scan and how scared I had been back then. Now it was different: I was no longer scared of the procedure. I was scared of getting bad results.

I left the hospital with the same feelings as I when went in, but a huge sense of relief overcame me on the drive home. I knew what science could do regarding this disease, and I had taken good care of myself during my treatments. The rest was out of my hands, and the answer now lay with my test results.

Once I got home, I e-mailed my doctor to let her know that I completed my follow-up lab and scan appointments. She replied within minutes to let me know she would contact me tomorrow once the results were in. That night I slept soundly, knowing I had done exactly what my doctors had recommended, and with faith in myself, knowing that I could beat this disease. My plan that night was to stay in bed until my doctor called me the next day. I was physically and emotionally drained by the whole process and knew I needed rest for the upcoming day.

So much for sleeping in, I woke up again early the next morning, and a sense of calm came over me. I knew I was going to get my results that day, but I wasn't as anxious as I thought I would be. I did say a little prayer and asked for strength as I prepared to receive any news with which my doctor would call me. I carried on with my morning doing light chores, and I even found gratitude in that, as I remembered being sidelined after my surgery and unable to even do my own laundry.

My doctor called me in the early afternoon. I looked at the phone, put down the laundry, took a deep breath, sat down, closed my eyes, and answered. She was always so calm whenever I spoke to her, which put me at ease, but this time she was excited as she eagerly said, "Valerie, your labs look great, your cancer marker is within normal range, your CT scan is clear, and there is no evidence of disease!" I opened my eyes, smiled, and let out a huge sigh of relief. My waiting-to-exhale moment had finally arrived! I smiled the biggest smile. She then added, "Congratulations, you are in remission."

I put her on speakerphone and asked her to repeat what she told me. I had to confirm that I wasn't dreaming it or had misunderstood her, and most importantly, I wanted Jett and Cisco to hear what she said. She repeated it, and they couldn't stop yelling with excitement and continued their cheering while I was still on the phone. I thanked her for all her help and for taking such good care of me. I started to cry. It was a happy cry, a cry that I hadn't had in a long time and had been waiting to let out for so long.

Before she hung up, she explained that I would have scheduled follow-up appointments for at least the first five years that would include blood draws and CT scans. This would continue until I was out of remission and considered "cured." I told her I wouldn't want it any other way, and with that, I kissed cancer goodbye. I could not wait to call my family and friends and tell them the good news and to thank them for all their support. I was ready to celebrate kicking cancer's butt and being in remission—but my celebration was going to be cut short.

PART III

A Citizen of Both Kingdoms

CHAPTER 7

"Mom! I'm officially in remission! There are no more signs or symptoms of cancer!" I said to her as soon as she answered the phone.

She asked me to repeat it and then asked me for the doctor's exact words. She let out a huge happy sigh of relief and thanked God profusely, then excitedly told my dad who I heard yell over the phone with happiness, "All right, Val!" She told me that she would cook dinner for all of us that night.

My brother, Brandon, and my sister-in-law, Shana, were just as excited, and my nephew and niece, Riley and Reese, gave me a big hug, even though they were too young to understand what was happening. I understood that it meant I would be around to see them grow up, God willing!

I called Sam and said, "Sam, we did it, we beat cancer!" I could almost see her smile over the phone as she said, "I knew you would!" She came over right away to give me a big hug.

That night we all had dinner at my mom and dad's home and celebrated. I couldn't thank them enough for their support, and I let them know I couldn't have done it without them. I was so excited to get control over my life again and not have to worry about taking my chemo pills or wondering what week it was and if I had to get my infusion that week and what side effects would surface. It all felt surreal. Six and a half months had been a long time for this disease to put a pause on my life. I was ready to press play and get back to living my best life in the kingdom of the well, but it wasn't that easy.

In those quiet moments in between celebrating my remission, I would hear this voice that would ask, "Why me? Why was I able to beat this disease when so many people haven't?" There are so many cancer warriors who have preceded me, and because of different circumstances sometimes out of their control, they didn't receive the same positive news as I did. Why was I able to live and continue with my life and be with my family? This was something that would always bother me, especially when I would hear about friends and their family members who had faced tough battles with cancer and succumbed to the disease. I dubbed this inner voice my warrior guilt. From what I understand, it's a normal feeling, but it was hard for me to manage, and it came up whenever I heard the word "cancer" or about someone being diagnosed with it.

Then one day I met up with my good friend Holly. She wanted to celebrate and congratulate me on the news of my remission. She excitedly asked me where I was going to travel to celebrate this monumental milestone event. She knew that I had been disappointed that I was unable to travel with my friends to South America the year I was diagnosed, so she thought I would choose South America as my first destination post-cancer. I told her that I planned to just lie low, as I was still a little concerned that the cancer might come back. She looked at me very skeptically and asked me if this was a concern that my doctors had about my health. I explained to her that it wasn't, and it was more of a concern that *I* had and that I was scared. She let out a huge sigh and then went on to remark that this seemed out of character for me. She said she thought that I would have plans for a celebratory trip somewhere by now. She went on to tell me that cancer was just a chapter in my life, and I shouldn't be defined by it nor give it any control over my plans for the future. I shouldn't let fear of the disease stop me from being who I am and experiencing all that I want to in life. She reminded me of my love of travel and about all the fun I had on my adventures. Holly has always been so honest and forthright with me, and that is something I truly admire and appreciate about her. She also said something else that really resonated with me: that no one is promised tomorrow and that being in remission was a huge accomplishment, so I should get out there and celebrate it. Sometimes you just need a swift kick in the butt like that from a good friend to set you straight.

I had to examine why I was feeling that way and after some soul-searching, concluded that when you have been given a second chance, you shouldn't take it for granted. I knew inside that I wasn't the same person I was pre-cancer. I saw things through a new lens that showed me how precious everything in life was—especially life itself, whether your own or a loved one's. Knowing that this disease affects everyone you care about makes you not want to take life for granted. It struck home for me that I should celebrate every little milestone in life—and being in remission was a *big* milestone. I remembered a promise that I made to myself at the beginning of my journey, that when I came out of my treatments, I wanted to continue traveling and experiencing all the different places, people, and cultures that the world has to offer. Life is so short, I had plans to see it all! Holly had reminded me of that promise to myself.

The next day I booked a trip to Hawaii for the following week. After all, paradise sounded like the perfect place to celebrate being in remission. I needed to feel that warm *aloha* spirit on the beach—drink in hand, sun on my face—and to just learn to relax and enjoy life again. Cisco, who I knew needed a break from it all too, was excited for our first trip to Hawaii together. Our friend Victor, a resident of Oahu, was happy we had chosen the Aloha State to celebrate my NED, "no evidence of disease," news. He surprised us with a limousine waiting for us at the airport to take us to the hotel, and when we were checking in, he surprised us again—he had upgraded our room to an ocean-view suite. See what I mean about that aloha spirit! I felt like I had leveled up my celebration in paradise.

That vacation was exactly what I needed to recharge, put everything into perspective and regain control of my life post-cancer. It was a necessary reflection period, one that made me realize that I shouldn't live in the shadow of cancer and that I should concentrate on life beyond this disease and all the adventures and happiness life brings. I was able to realign my internal compass to my true north and get back to all that is important in my life.

Two weeks after receiving my great news about being in remission, everything was slowly starting to get back to normal, and I was already back at work. It was an exciting time, and I felt ready to get back into the swing of things. It was my first real step back into the familiarity that had been suddenly taken away from me six months ago. I went back to work with a new set of eyes, seeing information, people, experiences, and especially work in a whole new light—as a patient. It wasn't just a career or business as usual for me. My job was with a purposeful company that serves patients with life-saving treatments that I now truly appreciated as an employee and as a recipient of our medications. I couldn't wait to go back and thank all my colleagues for what they do for cancer patients—I was living proof that the drugs we develop really do have a positive impact on patients' lives. There was a noticeable spring in my step as I started to see my colleagues around campus. I smiled harder, hugged deeper, and laughed louder. We were all in together, this search for a cure for cancer! Their compassion for patients and passion for their work inspired me to be the best I could be, in efforts to achieve epic outcomes for patients. They were just as excited to see me back in the saddle and ready to tackle new work-related challenges.

It was a busy four weeks of celebrating my NED, going out to dinner and drinks with family and friends and making plans for the future. Looking back, it was such a carefree moment as I made plans and didn't have the weight of my health to consider. For a whole month after my NED, I would wake up content and say to myself, "I did it . . . I beat cancer." Kingdom of the well, here I come!

Then I was blindsided. My mom invited Cisco, Jett, Brandon, Shana, and me over for dinner, an invitation we happily accepted, as we always enjoy her cooking. After a great dinner, my dad handed me a piece of paper from the Veterans Affairs (VA) hospital. He's been a member of the VA healthcare system since he served in the Navy. As I opened up the letter, I realized that it showed the results of a medical exam. I asked him what it was, and he explained that he went to the doctor's office about two weeks ago, and I didn't hear the rest, as I continued reading the letter and soon recognized that it contained results from a biopsy exam. By now, I was able to read lab results and biopsy results. I scanned the paper to the middle of the page, and my eyes landed on the words "positive for esophageal cancer."

Once again, the rug was completely pulled out from underneath me. In shock and at a loss for words, my eyes started to well up with tears as memories of my diagnosis came flooding back, and I became overwhelmed with thoughts about my dad enduring such a tough treatment plan. Overcome with confusion and concern, I asked again, "What is this?"

My dad explained again that a few weeks back, he felt a little lump in his throat and went to have it checked out by the doctors. They had performed an endoscopy—a flexible tube equipped with a video lens (video endoscope) was put down his throat and into his esophagus. Using the endoscope, the doctor examined his esophagus, looking for cancer or areas of irritation. The doctor found a growth in his esophagus and decided to have it biopsied. My dad said he really hadn't paid it too much attention since the lump didn't hurt, but he had just wanted to get it checked out to see if it was anything of concern. Silence overcame all of us.

My world turned upside down once again. Cancer had decided to reenter my world—and this time mess with my dad. I know firsthand how hard it is to comprehend being diagnosed with such a terrible disease and all the questions that run through your mind. I was able to ask my doctor questions right after my diagnosis, I couldn't imagine receiving the news via letter and not having all my questions answered. He had received the letter the day he showed it to us, so I knew the questions were brewing for him—actually, the questions were brewing for all of us. I looked at my mom and brother and saw the same, all-too-familiar looks on their faces as when I had told them about my diagnosis. I couldn't imagine how they felt going through this twice in less than a year with two different family members. I broke the silence by letting them know that I would call his doctor the next day to inquire about the letter and to confirm the diagnosis. I couldn't believe this was happening again to our family so soon after my battle.

I was able to get in contact with his doctor, and he confirmed that my dad's biopsy came back cancerous and that my dad had been diagnosed with esophageal cancer. My parents were present as I made the call, so the doctor explained to us that they wanted to do a PET scan (positron emission tomography scan), which is a procedure to find malignant tumor cells in the body. Determining the appropriate treatment would be dependent on the outcome of the PET scan. He scheduled a follow-up appointment for us to ask any questions we might have after the PET scan results were in.

The doctor continued to explain to us that there would be a few options to consider depending on the PET scan results. Chemotherapy and/or radiation would be required to shrink the tumor, followed by surgery to remove the cancerous tumor. This news rocked me to the core, as I know how hard chemotherapy is to endure, and adding radiation to the equation would only make it that much harder. In addition, my parents are in their seventies. Would my dad be able to handle such a tough treatment plan, and would my mom be able to take care of him? Of course, my brother and I would be there to help, but just knowing the day-to-day mental anguish this disease brings made all of us pretty nervous. We were still hopeful for a good outcome, and we scheduled his PET scan for late March.

We were all still in a state of shock, but my dad told us not to worry because we didn't yet know the PET scan results. Although I appreciated his approach, we still couldn't help but worry. We kept those worries between my mom, my brother, and me since we didn't want to add to my dad's already-full plate.

March finally came around, and my mom and I accompanied my dad to his PET scan appointment at the VA. It was such a different experience from mine at the HMO hospital, as the VA benefits are established by federal law and regulations and funded through appropriations. Although I did know the process of navigating through an HMO healthcare system from my own experience, the VA system seemed foreign to me, and I had to learn how a different system operates. Luckily, the staff was more than happy to meet with my mom and me regarding all the questions we had about his care. Once my dad checked in, the doctor came out to let us know that the results of the scan would take about a week and they would let my dad know via a call and a letter. Because we already knew that the biopsy was cancerous, we knew what the next steps would be, but we were hopeful that the scan would show minimal cancer cells and prayed that the chemotherapy and radiation combo would be the last resort.

While waiting for my dad to finish up with his scan, my mom and I left the hospital and decided to go for a walk on the beach. The San Francisco VA hospital is located right near Ocean Beach and has one of the most beautiful views of the Pacific Ocean. I think my mom and I just needed to walk to relieve some of the worries and stress that we were experiencing brought about by my dad's diagnosis. During our walk, she broke the silence first and said to me, "You know, Val, your dad is really strong, and he will be OK." Not only was she trying to reassure me, but I also think it was her way to reassure herself too. I know this approach all too well!

I smiled and said, "Who do you think trained me for my surgery and chemo?" I reminded her of when I was little when he would secretly teach me uppercut and jab boxing combinations in the basement while she thought he was teaching me how to roller-skate. We laughed and smiled at each other, then she put her hand on my back and said, "Let's go pick up your dad."

My dad took on his scan like the champ that he is! Immediately afterward, he was asking the doctors about the next steps, and they answered some of his questions. The doctors commented on my dad being so outgoing and positive. It's just how my dad is—he likes to make friends with people and always likes to know their names, especially the receptionists and nurses. I knew how this disease worked and the toll it takes mentally, and I hoped that his positive attitude would continue throughout his journey. We left the hospital hopeful yet nervous about the results.

In April, we received a call from the hospital, and they gave us the news that the PET scan results and multiple other tests my dad had taken all led to a recommended treatment course of chemoradiation, a combo of chemotherapy and radiation with a surgery scheduled afterward. The news was another blow to us, and we tried to stay positive and hopeful for my dad as the medical team discussed plans for his treatment. They recommended chemoradiation for a five-week treatment before surgery to try to shrink the tumor to make it easier to remove during surgery. The doctor went on to tell us that the recuperation time would take a while, as my dad would have to be in the hospital for about a week, then on a feeding tube for a month after that.

When it came time to answer my dad's questions, I knew he wanted to know what type of side effects or adverse reactions he would be up against during his treatments. I also knew he wanted to know what his diet would need to be like as he felt he needed to prepare for that. When the doctor told me about the potential side effects he may experience, it was somewhat similar to mine, except his included skin changes in the area where he was receiving the radiation, including redness, blistering, and peeling. As far as his diet, there weren't any restrictions just so long as he could keep things down. He was told that he should eat smaller, more frequent meals if he could. After the surgery, there would be a lot more food restrictions with the feeding tube, but he didn't want to know those at the moment as he was concentrating on taking it one step at a time—though I could tell his concerns were still there, as with all of us. My dad was very appreciative that I was able to get all his questions answered and I added my insight as to the side effects that he may or may not experience. I tried to downplay those side effects, but he had seen exactly what I went through—so much for downplaying that. I did let him know that the doctors said that everyone experienced chemo differently, so those side effects the doctor discussed with us were just guidelines of what people typically have and not everyone experiences the same. We left the appointment feeling more informed and less agitated.

I wanted him to feel comfortable with the entire process, so I discussed his anxiety around the disease and treatment with him and my mom and tried to answer their questions from my perspective, and if I didn't have the answers, I would call the physician. My speaking to his physician put him at ease, so I did it whenever he needed me to. Sometimes just letting him know that everything would be OK, God willing, was enough. He had seen firsthand what I went through, so he understood it from a caregiver perspective already, which was something about which I had no idea, only knowing it from a patient perspective. We would be teaching each other a lot.

Although I knew a lot about colon cancer treatments and chemotherapy, my dad had esophageal cancer, and radiation treatment was something I had no idea about. The word alone was scary, but I felt I had to get educated so that I would know how to best help him. I expressed my interest to learn more about my dad's disease and treatment to his physician, and he informed me that the hospital had consultation classes that I could attend so that I would get a better understanding of the process and care needed after my dad's treatments. I was more than happy to attend these classes and learn more about the disease—I saw that as the easy part. My dad would have to do all the hard work. These classes were so valuable to me as a caregiver, they armed me with knowledge about the disease, and I was better equipped to speak to my dad's doctors to clarify some of our questions. He felt more comfortable asking me, his daughter, certain questions than his physician, which is pretty normal. I didn't mind as it gave me insight into how he was dealing with it.

My dad also had some other minor medical issues that they wanted to resolve before his treatment start date, so we would have to wait until midsummer. Although I could tell my dad was worried, the doctors reassured him that the minor issues needed to be dealt with first and that there were no concerns about delaying his cancer treatment. My mom, brother, and I rallied behind him as he started the smaller treatments and procedures.

April to July seemed to take forever as he finished up those treatments. My dad understood the severity of cancer and wanted to start the protocol as soon as he could, which I completely understood. The wait from my diagnosis to my first treatment, the colectomy surgery, was only days and not months like my dad. He was frustrated, as he wanted to get it over with. I had to explain to him that with any cancer diagnosis, each treatment has a different journey. This was confirmed by his doctors, as they would check in with him every two weeks to make sure all his underlying conditions were taken care of so he would be strong enough for the chemoradiation treatments.

Thinking back to the days before my surgery, I really hadn't had time to dwell on the procedure itself. I barely had time to prepare for it, and to be honest, the fast pace of how everything unfolded worked for me. If I had been given more time prior to my surgery, I would have spent a lot of it worrying about the procedure. My dad, on the other hand, had about two and a half months to think about it, and so this led to a lot more "what if?" questions, which can spiral someone into a dismal state of mind.

He would ask me almost every time I spoke with him about my treatments and the side effects I experienced. I know he was questioning his strength through this uncertain time, so I tried to comfort him as best as I could and told him that the one thing I knew that would be constant was our family's support during this time and that we would be there with him every step of the way. It was something that needed to be said constantly because it eased our anxieties.

It was explained to us that combining chemotherapy and radiation treatments increases the likelihood and severity of side effects—which added to his frustration. I found myself visiting my mom and dad a lot more during this time to ease their worries about the upcoming treatments and also play the liaison between the doctor and my family. This was something I was more than happy to do, as I wanted to know how to ease their concerns.

My mom and I accompanied my dad to a few appointments before the start of his treatment. He understood that mine had been a different treatment since we had different diagnoses, but I think knowing that I had gone through something similar just recently eased his concerns. The doctors were more than happy to have my mom and me present at his appointments. At one of the earlier consultations, the doctor had informed us that the radiation treatments would be done at another hospital because the VA wasn't equipped with a radiation machine. With the Bay Area being so vast, the doctors reached out to a few hospitals in the area to check on the availability of a radiation machine for his use, and we waited to hear which hospital he would go to for his radiation treatments.

We found out a few weeks later that UCSF Medical Center at Mission Bay had a radiation machine that would be available for my dad to undergo his treatments. They scheduled an orientation with us so that we could get acquainted with the campus and the staff. It was a hot sunny day in June, and my mom, my dad, and I ventured out to San Francisco for my dad's consultation. The hospital was brand new at the time and just beautiful, you could smell the new furniture and fresh paint. As all three of us sat in the new exam room waiting for the doctor to come in. My mom and I could tell my dad was getting nervous—to be honest, we were all a little nervous.

The doctor came in and introduced himself and, I guess, sensed our nervousness as we introduced ourselves, as he offered to give us a tour personally so that we would feel a little more at ease under his care. The facilities were state of the art, and the staff were so friendly and accommodating, answering all our questions. We were also able to see the radiation machine, and somehow it didn't look as daunting in the big bright new room. After the tour, we were led back to the exam room, where the doctor gave us more information about the radiation treatment. He explained that the type of radiation my dad would receive, external-beam radiation therapy (EBRT), was a type of radiation therapy used most often for people with esophageal cancer. The radiation is focused on the cancer from a machine outside the body. It is much like getting an X-ray, but the radiation is a lot more intense. He would receive these treatments five days a week for five weeks.

Being diagnosed with a disease is frustrating, and not being able to understand all the cancer jargon that is spoken in the hospital and by all the doctors can get confusing and debilitating. I wanted to help my dad by attending all his doctor appointments, which I hoped would put him at ease about the entire process. During this consultation, the information was just too much for him to take in, and I could see him start to get agitated with the overload of information. I could understand how it could be so overwhelming, especially when the physician was explaining his entire regimen from the start to the recovery after his surgery. It was a lot to digest, but because I somewhat understood the overall process and the medical verbiage, I knew I would be able to continue the appointment with just my mom by my side. I told my dad that it would be OK if he stepped out and took a break, we would fill him in with all the details when he came back. He appreciated that and took a short walk around the hospital. I asked all the pertinent questions that I knew my dad would have wanted answers to, along with questions that typically only a cancer warrior would be able to ask.

My dad's radiation treatments were scheduled at UCSF, and his chemo treatments were scheduled at the VA hospital. Those hospitals are at opposite ends of the city, which was a concern for my brother and me. My parents were pretty independent and active: They still drove and would go out often to run their own errands and go grocery shopping. My dad was adamant that he would be able to handle going between hospitals, but I let him know that he would be too weak to drive and that Brandon or myself would pick him up, accompanied by our mom. We hated to take that independence away from him, but the safety risk of him driving himself to treatments was too great. After much debate, and with the help of his doctor, we were able to convince him that being driven to and from his treatments would be the best option. We were all on board to help my dad in any way we could. I was working full time, and I contemplated taking a leave from work to make sure his recovery would go smoothly and to ease the burden on my mom. I discussed it with my brother and my dad's doctors, and we decided to take a wait-and-see approach, as my dad was still strong and might not require too much help.

With that, the doctor scheduled his appointments for all five weeks, and my brother and I figured out our schedule and the days we would alternate to take him to his treatments. The countdown had begun, and my dad would start treatments for his cancer in one month. He felt prepared and was ready. Let *his* round one begin. *Ding-ding!*

CHAPTER 8

On July 4, we were celebrating Independence Day, as we always do, with a barbecue at our house with my entire family. It was such a good day. We spent the afternoon together and planned to light fireworks with the kids—Jett, Riley, and Reese—when the sun went down. My parents usually leave early before the fireworks start because they don't like to drive at night, but this year my mom chose to stay and see the fireworks with us. In the back of our minds, we knew dad's chemoradiation would start at the end of the month, but just for the day, no one mentioned it, as if to give it no more power than it deserved, and we all enjoyed the day despite knowing we all would be going into battle soon. My dad went home early to rest, while my mom stayed back and enjoyed the fireworks with us. It was such a joy to see her having fun with the kids.

On July 11, Cisco and I were at home watching TV when I received a call from Sam. She lived in an in-law unit attached to my parents' home and must have heard some commotion coming from upstairs where my parents lived. She said urgently, "I'm taking your parents to the hospital. Something is going on with your mom."

Frantically, I asked her, "What happened? Is everything OK? Did she suffer another stroke?"

In the past, my mom had suffered from mini strokes, from which she always recovered. Sam said she didn't know, so I told her I would meet them at the hospital. I looked at Cisco with concern as he had heard the entire conversation and was already grabbing his keys. He said, "Let's go." I was quiet on the ride to the hospital as I said my prayers in silence.

As Cisco and I entered the emergency area of the hospital, we saw Samantha in the waiting room speaking to a nurse. They informed me that they had rushed my mom into the emergency room and my dad had followed behind her. As I was escorted back into the emergency room, I saw my mom barely conscious, with an oxygen mask on, lying on the gurney. There were two nurses still positioning the medical monitors on her body and my dad by her side looking more concerned than I had ever seen him and holding her hand. I ran to her and held her other hand and said, "Mom, are you OK?" She barely opened her eyes and started to mumble something that I couldn't understand, but her hand lightly grasped mine as I started to cry. A flood of emotions overcame me as I desperately told her, "Mom, wake up, we are all here waiting for you, and we love you." Again, she tried to open her eyes and to speak, but no words left her mouth.

I looked at my dad and asked him what was going on, and he said, "They think she suffered another stroke."

One of the nurses turned to me and said they will need to run some tests on her to confirm what had happened. Another nurse came in and said that there are only two people allowed in the emergency room with a patient and that my brother was in the waiting room. I left the emergency room so that he could see her and sat in the waiting room with Sam and Cisco, crying and feeling despondent. I had more questions than answers.

My brother was only in the emergency room with her for a few minutes before they had to rush her up to the MRI department for a head scan. He was able to speak with the doctor and confirmed she might have suffered another stroke. I sat in the waiting room with everyone, sobbing as we waited for the results.

It seemed like forever, and I couldn't tell you how long we actually waited, but every time the door would open in the waiting room, we anxiously looked up to see if it was her doctor with the results. Everyone was somber yet still hopeful that the results would be positive. I again said my silent prayers and pleaded to God that she would come out of this OK. After a long while, the doctor came into the waiting room, and we immediately rushed to him for the results. He confirmed our worst fear by telling us that my mom suffered a bilateral stroke. He went on to explain that it's a rare event that can occur from multiple strokes on both sides of the brain or, in a unique circumstance, when a stroke in one hemisphere affects the other. He informed us that she would be admitted into the intensive care unit (ICU) that night. Deep sadness overcame me as I broke down once again, bawling with pain. It was another tough blow that life had handed to me and my family—one we didn't see coming. This time the strokes had hit her from both sides of her brain.

When she was admitted to the ICU, I stayed with her most of the night, as did my dad, my brother, Samantha, and Cisco. We all wanted to be there when she woke up. My dad finally had to tell us in the wee hours to go home and get some rest, he would call with any updates. Reluctantly, I did go home, but rest wasn't something I could do. I was consumed with worry and wanted to go back to the hospital to be there with her.

The following day, my dad, my brother, and I worked out a schedule to have one of us there by her side at all times. It was tough, as we all wanted to be there, but with my dad's cancer, we knew he needed his rest. We were at her bedside for two days praying for a miracle when the doctors said that the prognosis did not look good and they wanted to put her on life support. That hit us hard, and we were inconsolable that day. My dad told me to contact our relatives to let them know what was going on with my mom.

Over the next few days, my entire family, including aunts, uncles, and cousins, came by to visit my mom, pay their respects and wish for a miracle. On those days, I really felt how loved she was and would hear stories from her visitors of how caring she was to them and about the special moments they had shared with her.

Sadly, my mom never regained consciousness, and it was on July 18 that the doctors said we had to decide on whether or not to continue to keep her on the breathing machine. It was one of those soul-searching decisions that had to be made quickly because we did not want to see her suffer any more than she had to. I remembered that she had a will in place that contained her medical directives, so I frantically went over to my parents' house to search for it. There it was in her file cabinet, tucked in where she would keep all her important papers. When I opened up her will to the medical tab, there was an advance directive that included a do not resuscitate (DNR) order. I read it over and over again, trying to understand it. It was a simple directive that I just didn't *want* to comprehend.

I felt so conflicted inside, as selfishly, I wanted to keep her on life support and hope and pray for a miracle, but as I read the order, I could hear her voice reading it to me, and I started to cry uncontrollably. I thought about my dad not having his wife by his side throughout his treatments and could not make any sense of it. There were so many tough decisions I've had to make in my life, but this one was, by far, the hardest.

When I finally mustered up the strength to return to the hospital where my dad and brother were by her side, I sat down next to them, clutching her will and told them about the DNR order. They looked up at me and said that they knew but somehow couldn't bring themselves to tell me, as I had been adamant about keeping her on life support and that I needed to find that DNR for myself and come to terms with it. Seeing the order and just imagining her reading it to me, it became clear what we had to do. She had made the decision, and we had to respect it.

We called her parish priest to administer the last rites and her final anointing. As he left, the medical staff gave us a few minutes with her to say our last goodbyes. A pain unimaginable overcame my entire family, as life once again dealt another devastating blow, and we took her off life support. I held her hand until the very last moment of her life. My mom passed away on July 19. It was my birthday. It was on this day that she gave birth to me, and on this day, she received her wings in heaven.

Preparing for her funeral while getting ready for dad's upcoming chemoradiation treatment—which he still insisted on continuing on schedule—was so difficult. I called his oncologists to let them know what had transpired, and they agreed that he should postpone the start of his treatments, and they would touch base with us in two weeks to assess if we were all prepared mentally and emotionally for his treatments. I had a discussion with my dad to let him know that even though he wanted to start the treatments on schedule, that it would be best for his health to postpone for a few weeks. Once he understood that the doctors had recommended postponing his treatments, he finally agreed that it would be for the best. I suppose he wanted to continue with the schedule to keep his mind off my mom's passing. I could sympathize with this, and I told him we would be there for him, regardless, but that he needed to take this time to grieve and prepare for his treatments.

It was such an emotional time for me and my entire family, especially my dad, who had just lost his wife and was on the verge of starting his chemoradiation treatments. We would always look to my mom for advice, a sense of safety and soundness. As the rock of the family, she always knew what to do. Now we would be forced to see my dad's journey through without her. I was praying for courage and strength and had to reassure my dad that my brother and I would be right by his side every step of the way—no one should fight this awful disease alone.

In the days after my mom's passing, we made plans for her funeral arrangements. Brandon and I knew that my dad wasn't well enough to make those decisions on his own, so we took that on ourselves and with the help of a funeral service and our extended family, who reached out to us with support and advice. My Auntie Rose was the first to call me when my mom passed to send her condolences and also to inform me of a plot that my mom had purchased a few years ago. She told me to look through her file cabinet to find those documents. She told me, "Your mom didn't want to burden you or Brandon with the cost of her plot." That's in tune with my mom's humble and unselfish character, as she never wanted to burden anyone with anything she thought she could handle herself. I thanked my auntie for the information and advice and, once again, went searching through her file cabinet.

Once I found the document, it proved my aunt correct—my mom had purchased a plot at Cypress Lawn Cemetery in Colma. This was a relief for me, as I didn't have a clue where to start as far as planning my mom's funeral, and yet there she was guiding me from above. I contacted the funeral home where her plot had been purchased and let them know we needed to make plans for her celebration of life. Brandon and I had to make some quick decisions as far as the visitation and rosary, funeral mass, flowers, and reception. As we worked with the funeral company, we agreed that her visitation and rosary would be held on July 24 with her mass and interment the following day.

It was a quick five days from her passing to her funeral, and a lot of details needed to be handled, such as picking out her clothes, headstone, and casket; informing the family; and adding our special touch to the ceremonies. I helped my brother pick out photos for a slideshow he wanted to create for my mom's visitation and rosary day. It was a bittersweet day, looking back at all the photos with my dad and brother and reminiscing of all the good times we had as a family. I took on the responsibilities of informing our relatives, writing her eulogy, and designing the funeral program, which included an overview of her life. This took me down memory lane once again, as I recounted all her milestones and achievements that had made me feel proud to be her daughter.

On the morning of July 24, as I walked into the chapel where she lay in her casket, it was the first time I had seen her since her passing, and as I peered into the casket, she looked as pretty as I remembered her, with a very peaceful look on her face. Overcome with gratitude for all the sacrifices she had made for me in her life, I started to cry. I thanked her for everything that I am and will become. I vowed that her sacrifices would not be in vain and that I would make her proud.

Before long, family and friends from across the San Francisco Bay Area and as far south as Los Angeles started trickling into the chapel and were also overcome with sentiment as they watched Brandon's slideshow in tribute to her. It was about fifty or so photos that started with her as a child in the Philippines and went up through present-day pictures of our family and friends. It was beautifully done—no one could have done it better than Brandon. As the rosary started, I glanced to the back of the chapel and saw that it was at full capacity, with people standing in the back. It was a testament to how much she was loved and how she made all the lives she touched better.

Once the rosary was completed, it was time for me to give the eulogy. I knew it was going to be tough delivering my heart's message that I had tried to put into words. It was an honor that my dad and Brandon had asked me to deliver it, and I didn't want to leave any important aspect of her life out, especially the family and friends who have helped her along in life. For a moment, I felt the anxiety of getting it "right," but once on the podium, my heart silenced that anxiety. I was able to step up and give a heartfelt speech, with moments of crying along the way. I concluded the eulogy by thanking everyone for coming and informed them of the funeral mass, interment, and reception the next day. As the last one to leave that chapel that night, I said my goodbye to mom and said, "I hope I made you proud today delivering your eulogy. I love you, and I will see you tomorrow." Mournfully, I left the chapel and tried to get rest as I prepared for the next day.

The funeral director told our family to be at the chapel at 9:00 a.m. for the closing of the casket. This is typically reserved for the immediate family to say last goodbyes before the casket is closed and brought over to the church for the funeral mass. Cisco, Jett, and I picked up my dad and Samantha and headed over to the chapel, where Brandon, Shana, Riley, and Reese were outside waiting for us. My mom's three brothers and her nephew followed shortly behind us as they were her pallbearers. I knew this was going to be hard for everyone as this was going to be the last time we see my mom in person before they closed the casket. I was the first to walk up to her casket and say my private goodbyes, which included asking for continued guidance and strength for our family as we saw my dad through his treatments without her. After everyone said their goodbye in private, we stood all together and said a prayer as they slowly closed her casket. I felt my heart sink as I heard the casket lid thud close. The finality of seeing my mom for the last time hit me, and my eyes started pouring. I looked at the rest of my family, and there wasn't a dry eye in the room. I knew they felt the same.

As we left the chapel and our car followed the hearse to the church, it was calm and quiet as we consoled one another with hugs. As we stepped out of the car, we saw the rest of our family and friends outside the church, awaiting my mom's arrival for her last mass. Seeing everyone gather in honor of my mom had me in tears again, which lasted the duration of the mass. I remember walking into the church behind my mom's casket trying to comfort my dad by holding his hand while tears streamed down my face. It was one of the toughest hours to get through, knowing we would leave the church and travel to her final resting place.

It was during the homily that the priest said. "She is now at rest. She has found eternal peace in the kingdom of heaven."

I reflected on how much she must have suffered in the short time she was in the kingdom of the sick while in the hospital and found solace that now she was no longer suffering and was finally at peace. It was a beautiful homily, and as mass concluded, we followed my mom's casket down the aisle and into the hearse.

Once out of the church, my mom's hearse and the entire procession of about twenty-five cars had a police escort to her final resting place. Jett's father, Lee, had been able to get permission from the police department he worked for to do the escort for my mom, a gesture that my family and I were grateful for. As my mom's casket was taken out of the hearse, the priest said a few more prayers that I didn't even hear because I was too focused on my mom's casket being lowered into the ground and started to feel numb. As I placed my flowers on her burial site, I found comfort again in knowing that she will be helping us from heaven. We left the burial site and headed over to the reception, where we would meet the rest of our family and friends who had come to support us during our darkest days.

We had wanted her funeral to reflect how she touched so many lives during hers to be a beautiful celebration of her life. At the reception, my aunts and uncles came up to me and told me how everything was so beautiful and how much they will miss her. To this day, they tell me how much they still miss her. I think often about how she would tell me, "Leave people and places better than when you found them." I will, Mom, I promise.

CHAPTER 9

Two weeks after my mom's funeral, my dad asked me to call his oncologists and let them know he wanted to start his chemoradiation treatments for his esophageal cancer. My brother and I questioned if he was ready as he had just gone through the devastating and sudden loss of his wife. As I spoke with his doctors and voiced my concern about his readiness, it became clear that he was ready. As I have come to know from my own experience, when you are diagnosed with cancer, it affects you physically, mentally, emotionally, and socially. Your inner spirit rises and hope takes over—and not just selfishly, but because you want to live for your loved ones. No matter how hard it was for him to deal with my mom's passing—they were married for forty-seven years, and losing your partner after that many years is life-shattering—my dad was concerned with how hard it was for Brandon and me. He wanted us to stay hopeful and have faith that everyone was doing what they could to stay healthy, starting with himself. He *needed* to begin his treatments.

That week I took my dad to UCSF for a checkup with his doctor. They wanted to do an additional pre-chemoradiation consultation with him in person to make sure he was ready for the next five weeks of treatments and answer any questions we might still have. Physically, he is a strong man, but they wanted to evaluate how he was mentally and emotionally.

As we sat in the same exam room we had been in weeks ago with my mom discussing his treatment plan, we felt deeply her absence—she was so very missed. It was also apparent how much harder this journey would be for all of us. We sat in silence as we looked at the chair my mom had sat in the last time we were in that room. I finally had to break the silence, and holding back tears, I smiled at my dad and told him not to worry as she was still here, helping us from a higher place. He responded with a half smile, nodded, and said, "I know this."

The doctor came in and assessed my dad physically, then he started asking him if he was ready for the next five weeks. Dad let his doctors know that he wanted to start the treatments right away, as his late wife would want him to and that he wanted to live to see his grandchildren, Jett, Riley, and Reese grow up. I couldn't think of a better reason for him to fight. The doctor gave him a pat on the back and said, "You are more than ready for this." The doctor then turned to me and asked me if my brother and I were ready.

The question took me aback, as I questioned myself, *was* I ready? After all, my dad was ready, so shouldn't I be? Such a simple question with so many layers and most probably one of the most important questions that should be asked to all cancer warrior family members. Mental health is no joke when it comes to this disease, and to be completely honest, my own experience was that it's worse to watch a family or a friend go through their cancer journey than to actually go through it yourself. This was especially true for me, as I now could see it through both lenses, as a patient and as a caregiver. It would certainly be hard to see my dad go through his treatments and their side effects so quickly after my mom's passing. This disease takes a toll on the family and loved ones, and I so appreciated that the doctor asked us that question. So in short, my answer to the doctor was "yes," I was ready. After all, it was just six months ago that I had fought cancer and won. It had become my duty to be my dad's tour guide into the kingdom of the sick and help lead him back to the kingdom of the well, so I told his doctor, "The question should be, is cancer ready for *us?*"

I wanted to provide the same unwavering support for my dad that my mom had provided for me. I shared with my dad my firsthand knowledge about the disease, which I'd like to think bolstered his confidence. It wasn't something I could have lied about, since he had seen everything I went through during my treatments, but I did try to minimize it. I could see the concern in his eyes as he asked me questions about my side effects and how I dealt with them. To keep him thinking positively, my answer would be, "But I'm fine now." He would laugh—nervously. I did have to remind him that my treatments were over a six-month span and his were scheduled over five weeks, which is not to diminish or compare treatments but for him to see that the light at the end of the tunnel would be well within reach.

Insights into the disease and the treatments were something I could provide my dad at the very least for him to get a better understanding of what's to come. I took an approach of offering this information unsolicited, as I recognize that people process ambiguity differently. For me, I had wanted to know and understand all aspects of what I may or may not have to deal with during my entire cancer journey. I felt best prepared knowing the answers to all my "what ifs," so I continued to ask my doctors questions during the entire process, which they didn't mind.

For my dad, he dealt with things on a week-by-week basis, understanding that he was shouldering a lot emotionally. With my mom's passing being so recent, this approach worked best for him. He would map out his appointments on a calendar for the week so that he would know which hospital we would go to on which day and which treatments he would be receiving. It was a process he could control. On Mondays, he would check in with his doctor to understand what the regimen was for the week and any side effects he would potentially have during that week, and in turn, the doctor would also ask him which side effects he was currently experiencing and about his overall mental health around the treatments. This approach was ideal for him.

Our two different approaches to handling the information about his treatments worked for us. He preferred to be on a need-to-know basis for the week, and I preferred to have all the information at once. So as he progressed through the weeks of his treatments, I had a bird's-eye view of what was to come, and I felt well prepared as a caregiver, and he felt he had enough information for the week as a patient going through treatments.

His doctors appreciated this approach, and at one of his in-person appointments, my dad asked, "So, doctor, what can I expect this week as far as any side effects?"

The physician, who knew us all too well by now, said, "I think you can ask your daughter that."

I took out my trusty notebook and read from my notes, "Nausea and vomiting, diarrhea, painful sores in the mouth and throat, fatigue, pain with swallowing, dry mouth, or thick saliva."

My dad looked at the doctor and asked if I was correct with my list of potential side effects, and the doctor replied, "Yes, she is."

My dad replied, "Well, I have to prove her wrong again!"

That made for a good laugh. A laugh you could hear well outside the office we were in and a laugh that was needed to ease the anxiety of the upcoming week's treatments. Yes, please, Dad, prove me wrong!

So for the next five weeks, my brother and I took turns taking my dad to chemotherapy and radiation treatments at two different hospitals. It was exhausting at first, waking up in the morning and figuring out what day it was, which hospital to take him to and who was supposed to take him. He received twenty-five treatments of radiation, which was every weekday, not on weekends. I was still working full time and would take him during lunch or some days I would leave work early—the same would go for my brother.

Fortunately, on his radiation days, he only experienced minimal discomfort, which included tender skin and fatigue. The days he would receive the combination of chemotherapy and radiation treatment were the worst! On those combination treatment days, he would experience the tender skin and fatigue tenfold and would have some slight nausea, but nothing we couldn't handle. Some days he felt good enough to drive himself to get his radiation, and he did, but either my brother or I would follow him in our cars just to make sure he arrived safely to and from his appointment.

I knew that after my chemo appointments, I wasn't well enough to drive, so I was happy that he wasn't having those same side effects. I also knew how it felt to have all your independence taken away by this ugly disease. The doctors were OK with him driving himself to his radiation treatments, as long as he felt well enough. The days he had both treatments were definitely out of the question, and my brother or I took him to those appointments.

All in all, it was going well, as he was three weeks into his treatments with minimal side effects. I like to believe it's because of divine help from God and my mom. Dad made me look like a wuss when I was going through my treatments! The doctors at both hospitals would comment on how well he was doing during his appointments. Little did we know that the worst was yet to come.

He completed his five-week chemoradiation treatments nine days before his birthday, and then the doctors wanted him to physically recover before they performed the esophageal cancer surgery the following month. On the last day of radiation, there was a bell in the hospital that patients would ring once their treatments were all completed. Next to the bell, there was a plaque that read, "Ring this bell three times well, its toll to clearly say, my treatment's done, this course is run, and I am on my way!" He rang that bell like a champ! Afterward, he asked the doctors if it was OK for him to travel because he wanted to go to Las Vegas and try his luck on the slot machines for his birthday. He had a post-treatment appointment three days later, and they gave him the green light to travel.

The morning of the flight to Vegas, I remember being excited and waking up extra early—apparently, I wasn't the only one. My dad called me shortly after I woke up and told me he was on his way and would pick up breakfast for us so we could eat before our flight. I could hear the excitement in his voice. I think we were all ready to have some fun and let loose after months of endless medical appointments. Sam and Cisco came too, as they had been there for my family throughout the whole process, so it was only fitting for them to be there to celebrate the end of Dad's treatments. In fact, it would have seemed empty if they hadn't been there for the celebration. It was his first trip to Vegas without my mom, so I was a little worried about how he would feel not having her there.

As we sat on the plane, I remember looking at my dad as he was gazing peacefully out the window watching the clouds passing underneath us. I tapped him on his arm and asked him how he was feeling. He replied with a smile that I haven't seen for months and said, "I feel good, Val! I'm ready to win!"

It was the day before his birthday, so I replied, "Now wouldn't that be a great birthday present."

As we walked around the Las Vegas strip, our senses were filled with the flashing lights and sounds of the slot machines, the hot desert sun on our skin, and the enticing aromas from the nearby restaurants. Our worries seemed to melt away that weekend. We even joyfully reminisced about the last time we were in Vegas with my mom as my dad sat at her favorite slot machine and tried his luck. We were all pleasantly surprised when he won some money at her favorite slot machine. Happy birthday, Dad!

I felt my mom's presence that weekend as we celebrated the end of our chemo appointments, along with my dad's birthday at one of their favorite destinations, and I could feel her smiling down on us. My dad even chose to eat at their favorite buffet restaurant, the Paradise Garden Buffet at the Flamingo Hotel, for his birthday dinner. This weekend trip left us feeling recharged and re-energized as we flew back to the Bay Area.

Back at home, we were busy prepping for his upcoming surgery. Esophageal cancer surgery carries a risk of serious complications, such as infection, bleeding, and leakage from the area where the remaining esophagus is reattached to the stomach, so we had many pre-surgery appointments with his primary care doctor and oncologist. There were also a lot of labs that had to take place before surgery. My dad was in a good place mentally and physically, no doubt Vegas had helped. He wanted to beat cancer, and he knew that to do that, the surgery would be his final step in that process.

As his surgery day in October approached, my brother and I took the day off of work so that we could take him. On the day of, we all sat in the waiting room with anticipation for them to call his name and escort him into the surgery prep room. I looked at my dad, and I knew exactly how he was feeling. Those scary, anxious, and sad feelings prior to my colectomy surgery came rushing back to me. I put my hand on his and said, "It's OK, we'll be here when you get out."

It was the same words he had said to me as I went into my surgery. He smiled and said, "Everything will be all right."

He was then called into the preparation room, and the doctor came out to reassure us that he was in good hands.

The surgery was to take about four hours. My brother had to catch up on work, so I went for a walk on the beach, the same walk I had taken with my mom when we were waiting for my dad to finish up with his first PET scan a few months ago. I took that walk down memory lane because I knew I could find her there. On that walk, I asked her for strength for my dad: An esophagectomy is an open surgery where the goal is to remove all the tumor to prevent it from returning or spreading. I also prayed for strength for my whole family to help us all get through this surgery and the healing afterward. After my walk down memory lane with my mom, my brother called, and I met him to have a late lunch.

Before we knew it, four hours had passed, and we received a call to come back to the hospital as Dad was now out of surgery and in his recovery room. He was still asleep because of the meds, so we set up his room with pictures of his grandchildren and notes they had written to him to get well so that when he woke up, he would remember his reason to fight.

When he woke up, he was noticeably in pain and a bit disoriented. I fought back the tears and remembered how hard it was to wake up from my surgery, which was *before* my chemotherapy. His surgery was after his chemoradiation treatments, so I could only imagine how much harder his recovery would be. He called for the doctor right away and wanted to know what all the tubes were that were coming out of his body. It was a scary sight because there were tubes everywhere. The doctor explained to us what all the tubes were and also pointed out the feeding tube and the instructions for us for when Dad would be ready to go home. The doctor also explained that he would stay in the hospital for about five days to be closely monitored. My dad isn't one to be comfortable staying at hospitals, as he is a germaphobe and likes the comfort of his own home, but this time he didn't seem to mind as he knew he would be under close observation and the doctors would be only a few steps away if any complications were to arise.

During those five days he was recuperating in the hospital, Brandon and I visited him every day, and as caregivers to our dad, we had to take classes on how to use his feeding tube. This included information on how to care for the tube, inserting the food and administering his medications. As we took these classes, I wondered how he would feel being attached to this tube for a month. Would he be hungry—or even worse *hangry?* Would it feel strange for him to sleep with the tube in, let alone to be fed through it and not to be able to eat? Would it hurt him? Would my brother and I be able to manage it? Again, a lot of questions couldn't be answered until he was released from the hospital.

The day came when he was finally discharged, and it was apparent that we were all a little nervous about leaving the safety of the hospital and being under the care of the amazing doctors and nurses. Attempting this journey ourselves seemed a little overwhelming, but the doctors informed us that a visiting nurse would be available to us and would be stopping by every week for a quick check-in with my dad. This eased our anxiety a bit.

The first week was the most difficult, as we had to settle into a new routine. My dad was in so much pain from the surgery and with a feeding tube attached to his stomach, and there was no way he could be left by himself alone at home. I think I broke down and cried a few times from seeing him in so much pain and feeling frustrated with the whole process. I revisited taking a leave from work again, and I decided to discuss that option with my dad since we were all struggling. His response was "Absolutely *not*! What's wrong with you?" Those were his exact words. It did make me chuckle a little bit. He continued, "I'm not helpless! I'm just sidelined for a bit." Touché, Dad!

As I have stated before, my dad is a strong independent man and never wanted to be seen as helpless—after all, he was a boxer in the Navy. His active lifestyle was put on hold, as he didn't feel at ease leaving his home with a tube attached to him—totally understandable. I don't think he would have been able to enjoy himself, always having to adjust the tube in public. But if ever there was a time to be helpless, this would have been that time, and no one would have faulted him for that. As I found out, it's just not in his nature to act that way. He justified it further and said that my mom would echo his sentiments. He reminded me that the first week was always tough, referencing my first weeks of diagnosis, surgery, and chemotherapy. He was right, those first weeks were always the hardest. I thought back to when I was first diagnosed and how hard it had been for me and all the questions I had. Then I thought back to how my family must have felt, and it became a little more clear. The feelings I had toward my dad's first week of recovery were exactly how they were feeling when I was going through my treatments. And here I thought I was helping him, but he was teaching *me* how to be a caregiver!

He comforted me by saying that things would get better, that we had to have faith in the science and the process, and that everything would be just fine. He added that what we were currently doing worked with his recovery schedule. Brandon or I would go over to his house on our lunches and after work to help him, and that worked perfectly for him, he told me. He was able to rest and recover during the day. He went on to say, "What are you going to do here, watch me watch TV during the day?" OK, that made me laugh again.

He got serious again, saying, "Your efforts at work are important to you, and you need to keep your mind busy and not just focus on me and my health."

This was his way of telling me to keep my mental health in check. He also reminded me that we had been able to get through the worst, which was the first week after his surgery, so it would only get easier from here on out. With that, I continued to work full time and took days off as needed to help him when the visiting nurse came for his appointments. I hate to say it, but he was right. The rest of the three weeks became easier, as we settled into the groove and balanced work, life, and his care with a messy sort of finesse.

That first week home from surgery, my dad barely slept at night because he couldn't get used to the tube and had to keep adjusting his sleep positions, but overall, he said it wasn't too much of a bother and that he didn't feel hungry at all. I, on the other hand, was a little freaked out seeing a tube inserted into my dad's stomach and having to adjust the tape around it every now and then, not to mention taking the tube out to clean it to prevent clogs and reinserting it into his stomach area. But as the weeks went on and with the help of the visiting nurse lending me her expertise, it became easier. By the fourth week, we were happy to receive a call from the doctors letting us know that he was healing fine and that the feeding tube would be removed at the end of the week, with another PET scan scheduled for that month.

In the weeks after the feeding tube was removed, my dad regained his freedom and strength. He was able to do his normal activities outside of his home like grocery shopping and walking around Oyster Point Park in South San Francisco. He had his first PET scan post-surgery, and a few days later we received the results. We were ecstatic to find out that the PET scan showed NED. He had the same post-cancer instructions as me, with yearly checkups and scans, but the most important thing was that the chemoradiation and surgery worked, and he was now in remission. The strength within him had been greater than all the storms he had endured. This was my dad's waiting-to-exhale moment, and a few months later, we were back in Vegas celebrating life!

I had my dad choose the date for our trip back to Vegas, as I wanted to make sure he felt physically strong enough to travel and celebrate. The dates he chose were December 31 through January 2, and it couldn't have been more appropriate to usher in a new year by welcoming my dad back into the kingdom of the well. It also happened to be Samantha's birthday weekend, so it was a dual celebration. As Sam, Cisco, my dad, and I gathered on the Las Vegas strip on December 31 to watch fireworks and welcome in 2017, we had a celebratory toast like no other. We have always toasted to great health and happiness, but coming out of 2016 with all its challenges, this new year had a deeper meaning, and we were grateful to come out of it together and embrace 2017. It was even more epic than our last trip to Vegas. The lights seemed brighter, and the sounds more exhilarating, as this time we were celebrating the end of cancer and the start of our remission stage.

So that inner voice that used to ask me, "Why me? Why was I able to survive this terrible disease while so many people haven't?" was finally hushed as the answer became clear to me. I made it through so that I could help my dad and guide him through his journey. I told myself that I would do it for my dad and all the cancer warriors whose lives were cut short because of this disease. I'll live for them and make them proud that I was guiding another warrior through his journey back to the kingdom of the well. I understood that everyone had different paths when it came to this disease and no two journeys were the same, but it's one that I could help escort him through. After all, my dad had taught me uppercut-jab boxing combinations when I was a little girl to help protect myself, and I had taught him the uppercut-jab combinations that included a knockout punch right between cancer's eyes. After he was in remission, my gratitude deepened even more, as I was thankful to have my dad and myself survive this terrible disease with the help of all our family and friends.

Letting go of that "Why me?" guilt allowed me to grow exponentially as a person. It taught me to have a huge amount of respect for those cancer warriors that we have lost. It's not as though I knew the ins and outs of this disease and how to beat it, but I knew I could help guide my dad through it and be there for him with anything he may need. I put those feelings of guilt away for my dad and for all those cancer warriors who went before me, and I chose to be resilient. From his diagnosis to my mom passing away, chemoradiation, surgery, and his post-cancer appointments, my brother and I were there by his side every step of the way, and I had been able to give him the perspective of a cancer warrior fresh out of battle and to be his guide back to the kingdom of the well. Every great warrior must learn to endure and overcome—and my dad was definitely a cancer warrior!

CHAPTER 10

We struggled a lot that year, but dealing with the death of my mom was something we all helped one another with and still do to this day. It's hard enough to deal with one of your parents being diagnosed with cancer and the stress of managing that, but to have another parent pass away during the same time was a sadness that was unimaginable. We dealt with it day by day, and some days were better than others, but we got through it together. Coping with our grief was something we had to understand takes time, as healing happens gradually, and we allowed the process to naturally unfold for us. During those tough days, we would ask one another, "What would Mom do?" and then things just seemed to fall into place.

Life slowly returned to normal, but it was a different kind of normal. I guess you could call it the new-and-improved normal, with the knowledge that things would never be the same, but it was embraced by my dad and myself. I noticed this first with my dad. Back when he was in treatment, after his appointments, we would just stop and grab a couple of sandwiches for lunch on the way home and eat it at his house. But after his last appointment, he asked me if I was in a rush because he wanted to eat the sandwiches at the beach. I didn't know where this was coming from, but by no means was I going to argue. Lunch at the beach? Yes, please! So we picked up our sandwiches and drove to Ocean Beach to eat our late lunch. He talked about "Playland at the Beach" and how he and my mom would go there on dates. Playland was a seaside amusement park located next to Ocean Beach in San Francisco. It closed Labor Day weekend in 1972. After he reminisced about Playland and his dates with my mom, we walked to the ruins at Sutro Baths, another San Francisco landmark that is now part of the Golden Gate Recreational Area, and he reminisced some more. I guess he had to take his walk down memory lane to feel close to my mom again and to feed his soul. I enjoyed hearing all their stories, and it fed my soul as well as my heart. Her presence was strongly felt that day as we kept her memory alive.

Once my dad was in remission, he adjusted to life without my mom in his own way. He didn't have the opportunity to fully mourn her passing while he was going through his cancer battle, so his grief was most apparent when he was in remission. He came over a lot more to our home just to check up on us, to see how we were doing. On the weekends, he would do some gardening around our home, which was something he and my mom used to do every weekend. Gardening was exercise for him, he would say, but I think he just wanted to be around his grandchildren and reminisce about my mom. Who can blame him, as the stories made us all smile, and we enjoyed recollecting those happy moments we all had together. He would tell his grandchildren, "Your grandma loved you a lot!" as he would leave our house. It was good to see him active again and carrying those happy moments with my mom close to his heart and sharing those memories with the family.

His thank-yous seemed a lot more abundant after he was told he was in remission, and he vocalized them often. He had always been a grateful person and taught my brother and I to be thankful as well. It was funny to see him teach it to his grandchildren the exact same way he taught it to my brother and I, reminding them, "Always say please and thank you." I saw how living his life through the different lenses of a caregiver, patient, and widower had changed him. Although he had always been polite, it was more heartfelt after being in remission. For example, he had always enjoyed doing his own grocery shopping, and being a creature of habit, he would always buy the same foods. So when we would do our grocery shopping, we would pick out a few different things for him to try. You can tell he really appreciated it and was always enthusiastic and very grateful. His appreciation of food grew immensely, and I believe this was brought about by him not being able to eat solid food for an entire month—and who can blame him? He became a little adventurous with his eating and turned into somewhat of a simple foodie.

He eventually started to get into his old groove again and was feeling up to seeing his friends once more. Before his treatments, they would go on hikes on the Pacifica Trails near his home. It was their way of getting together and updating one another on their life's events while getting in some exercise. After a month in remission, he decided he was ready for this once again. I could tell he had missed it as he would call me excitedly afterward, letting me know how much fun he'd had and how far they'd hiked. Once he was well enough and ready, we rejoined our big Filipino family gatherings on holidays, which included all my aunts, uncles, and cousins. We had missed a few because of my mom's passing and my dad's treatments. It was noticeably harder on holidays, as anyone who has lost a family member will tell you, and we didn't want to rush him into anything he wasn't ready for. At those holiday family gatherings, it was apparent that we all missed my mom's delicious Filipino cooking and, most importantly, her joyful presence.

My dad and I were officially in remission and well on our path to be "cured." Some doctors use the term "cured of cancer" when referring to cancer that doesn't come back within five years. But cancer can still come back after those five years, so it's never truly cured. Don't get me wrong, I will take those five years and all the many years after that. As a cancer warrior, you always have that thought in the back of your mind, "What if it comes back?" I call this the cancer creep, and I mean this as a derogatory term—cancer *is* a creep—and to refer to how this doubt inches into your mind and takes over any hope you have of being forever cured of this terrible disease. This is where it gets tricky: Managing physical and emotional health around this is a delicate yet important balance.

For me, I tended to err on the side of caution when I was first told I was in remission, and I wanted to lie low and not take too many risks. For one, I had just finished a tough battle with cancer, and chemotherapy was something I never, ever wanted to do again. It was very tough on me physically, emotionally, and mentally, and it drained me at every chemo cycle that I went through. Two, I saw how hard it was for my family to see me go through this journey. They were constantly worried about my health. That cancer creep was certainly present in the beginning stages of my remission. The thought of cancer coming back someday without any warning was so ominous that I proceeded through life with caution and was very careful with my decisions. I basically played it safe but quickly learned—with the help of nudges from close friends and family—that this wasn't my true, authentic self. They reminded me of my love of life and travel. I couldn't let cancer take those things away from me, especially after being in remission, so again, I pivoted, and I am happy to say that I took control and lived my life without giving that cancer creep power over it.

There were times when the cancer creep would enter my dad's mind, and he just wanted to stay home a lot more than usual. Of course, there are times I felt this way too, and it's OK to stay there for a little bit and reflect, but one can't live in that dark place for too long as it is not beneficial for mental health. Everyone should have someone to lean on to help pull them out of that black hole and remind them of how far they have come and how much they have to look forward to. When I would see my dad start to worry, I would remind him that he is under constant care and being monitored by his doctors, so if something doesn't look right on his tests, they will let him know.

We were seen by our separate oncologists every three months for a complete blood workup, including checking our cancer markers, plus every six months we would undergo scans in which they would look for any new or recurrent tumors or masses. These tests were supported by conversations with our physicians about any new symptoms we may or may not experience. These safeguards helped him overcome his uneasiness over his return to the kingdom of the well until he was confident enough to fight that cancer creep off. Fear of cancer returning should not dictate how he or anyone who has this disease should live. For me, it was only in the beginning weeks of remission when that cancer creep had the most power. It would try to take advantage of my already-fragile state of mind. But as they say and as I learned, a well-lived life is the best revenge. I told my dad that to take that power away from cancer, we just had to keep on living our best life and not be scared of the "what if it comes back?" question but to think about "what if it *doesn't* come back?" I asked him, "What would you attempt to do if you knew cancer wasn't going to come back?"

He was quiet for a little bit, then he smiled, and I replied, "We should do that!"

We had this exchange often to remind us to look past that creep and to look forward to the things we wanted to do in life. We handled it differently, but the outcome was the same. I'm happy to say that he is living in retirement happy, healthy, and still as independent as ever— always looking forward to the next trip to Las Vegas.

In the years that followed, I was beamed with pride and joy to be able to see Jett graduate from high school and go away for college in Southern California. It was such a huge moment for me to see that his future was looking bright, and I was able to be fully present without that cancer creep hanging over me. Going away for college was something I had wanted to do when I was younger, and although it made me sad to see him leave, I knew this would be an awesome opportunity for him to grow and start his own adult experiences, plus knowing that he was only an hour flight away made it a little bit easier. I have to give Jett a huge amount of recognition and admiration for how he handled my struggle with cancer. It was tough for me as an adult to handle the difficulties with my dad, but Jett had to handle my struggle with this disease as a teenager. Watching his mom go through treatments, then suddenly losing his grandma, and then watching his grandpa being diagnosed with cancer took courage and strength well beyond his years. Another incredibly proud moment was when he told me he wanted to major in public health. Being around healthcare workers when my mom was in the hospital, through my dad's chemo treatments, and during my own battle helped solidify for him that he wanted to be a part of the healthcare sector. He stated that he wanted to be part of the solution. He's now entering his senior year at California State University at Fullerton, and I can't wait to see him walk the stage with his Bachelor in Science degree next year. Jett Magalong, you will do great things! You make us proud, and I know Grandma is smiling down on all your accomplishments.

Along with being able to see Jett graduate from high school and see him off to college, I also was blessed to be able to take him to Europe for his high school graduation, a place he had always wanted to visit. To be honest, I think I was even more excited than he was to travel with him to Europe and see all the wonder in his eyes as he experienced different countries and new cultures, broadened his horizons, and met new people with different perspectives and backgrounds than his own. We traveled through the Netherlands, Belgium, and France. This trip opened his mind to the world of travel. He caught the wanderlust bug and is already planning the places he wants to travel to after college—developing his own travel bucket list!

But Europe wasn't my first trip out of the continental United States post-remission. A few months after our celebratory New Year's trip with my dad to Las Vegas, Sam, Cisco, and I decided to take a cruise from Puerto Rico to the Southern Caribbean islands. It was a perfect trip to get my feet wet—no pun intended—and see how I felt about traveling so far away. The timing couldn't have been any better as my mind was finally at ease, with my dad and myself being in remission. It felt exhilarating to be able to travel outside of the United States and venture out to places I'd only seen in photos.

Our first stop on our cruise was St. Thomas, US Virgin Islands, and the beaches did not disappoint. As I lay on the white sand beach of Brewers Bay, looking out at the calm, crystal-clear waters framed by lush green hills on both sides, I felt once again the excitement of travel and the appreciation for the beauty of nature that had I missed while I was busy battling cancer. It was a rejuvenating experience, as I reflected on my treatments and how far I've come. I was thankful to be alive, and I couldn't wait to see the rest of the Caribbean Islands on our ports of call. This trip also re-energized my sense of adventure. While on the island of St. Maarten, we decided to go helmet diving. Helmet diving is where they put a seventy-pound helmet on you that looks like something an astronaut would wear and is equipped with air but no mouthpiece—the air is continuously flowing through the helmet. The weight of the helmet keeps you submerged so that you can walk on the ocean floor. It was a little overwhelming at first as they put this intimidating helmet on me and I descended a ladder to thirty feet below sea level, but once on the ocean floor, I got my bearings, and it was a magical experience to walk the ocean floor. Not only was I in a different country, but it felt like I was in a different world, experiencing the ocean scenery in all its beauty and serenity. That's exactly what this trip brought back to me: the beauty, serenity, and wonderment of life.

With my renewed excitement for traveling, I was able to continue my quest for the seven continents, and I was able to finally add another continent to the list: South America. Sam, Cis, and I were able to travel more than seven thousand feet above sea level in the Andes Mountains to see Machu Picchu in all its beautiful and grand glory. Sure, it's amazing to see it in pictures, but to experience it with my own eyes, standing on an Andean peak, gazing among the clouds while walking through thousand-year-old ruins was an experience that I was so grateful to finally have. But the best parts of the trip were experiencing the Peruvian people, their culture, and their delicious cuisine. It will go down in the books as one of my all-time favorite trips.

I just have one more continent on my bucket list to check off: Antarctica. Anyone down to take a South Pole vacation? Ha! Although I prefer to take warmer vacations, I hear the majestic beauty of Antarctica is like no other continent, and I can't wait to experience it one day.

I was so grateful that my father and I were in remission and had beaten that cancer creep so that it had no power over us and that I could continue to indulge my love of travel. It had taken a village to help us get back to the kingdom of the well, and that village included all our family members, friends, doctors, nurses, and lab techs. A sense of harmony and gratitude came over me, and I finally began to feel at ease with my re-entry into the kingdom of the well.

Then out of nowhere, another voice began to surface, asking me, "How are you going to show that gratitude now that you and your dad are in remission and living a healthy life?" That voice was telling me to give back just as people gave to my dad and me. It didn't stop there, it also made me think how I want to make a difference now that I was blessed to have my life back. I wasn't sure how, but I knew that I wanted to make an impact and give to those who might be lost in their own cancer journey.

PART IV

The Return to the
Kingdom of the Well

CHAPTER 11

I had come full circle with my own battle as a cancer warrior, and the gratitude began to run deep within me. I thought of my colleagues who had developed the drug that helped me beat this disease and all the help I had received from my family and friends to help me get back to the kingdom of the well, and I was overwhelmed with appreciation. I became more self-aware, and I searched for a way to show my appreciation by paying it forward. They say when you walk with gratitude, it heals your mind, body, and spirit—and helps attract more things to be grateful for. This could not have been more true for me. And although I still struggle with the loss of my mom to this day, I was grateful that my dad and I had been able to beat cancer, and we were living happy and productive lives in remission.

Upon my return to work, that voice that was asking me how I was going to show my appreciation and gratitude began to grow stronger. Soon a new position was posted for a rotational opportunity as a patient navigator. Although I wasn't too familiar with the drug that the position was designed around, I knew I wanted to see if I had it in me to give back to patients just as my patient navigator helped me.

A patient navigator is a health professional that focuses on the patient's needs. The navigator helps guide the patient through the healthcare system and works to overcome obstacles that are in the way of the patient receiving the care and treatment they require. It's a necessary role for traversing through the often difficult and confusing healthcare system.

During my care, I had a patient navigator who guided me at the beginning of my journey through the cost of care and helped me understand an overall snapshot of my treatments to come. My patient navigator helped me understand what was covered under my plan and if any assistance would be needed along the way. Fortunately, I had really good insurance coverage, and the only payment out of pocket was just a copayment for my surgery—the rest of my treatments were covered under my plan. I began to think about other patients who didn't have a similar plan and wonder if there was a process in place for them to receive treatments if they weren't covered.

Once I saw the patient navigator role posted, I found myself thinking about it all the time. I had been able to help my dad navigate through his healthcare journey, and I knew I wanted to give back to patients by sharing my insights about my own personal battle, being a patient and a caregiver. I received a few e-mails from colleagues letting me know about this opportunity and strongly suggesting that I should consider applying for this rotation. I appreciated all their support, but I thought to myself, was I ready? Was I ready to open myself up to those floodgates of emotion and put my own feelings aside to be able to help patients? The final push came from my manager at the time, Joni, who also forwarded the opportunity along with a note to let me know that although she would miss me on her team, that the opportunity aligned with my greater passion—to help patients—and it would be a mistake if I didn't apply. Now that's what I call looking out for someone's best interests—and with that, I applied.

A little background on Joni: I only worked for her for a few months before the rotational opportunity was posted. I knew her wife, Edith, first, as head of our biooncology department, and she had been instrumental in answering my questions regarding my chemotherapy medication. It was a friendship that came full circle, and I appreciate them so much for their help with my journey from pre- to post-cancer.

It was a pretty tough interview process for the patient navigator rotation. It consisted of a phone screen interview and once past that, a two-person panel interview. It was a two-week process, and you would be contacted at the end of the two weeks to let you know if you would be extended the offer for the position or not. Although it wasn't an oncology product and I had no clinical background, I was open and honest with the interviewers about my journey and let them know that I was a patient taking one of the products that we developed. I reminded them that all patients facing difficulty with a disease do need help to feel comfortable in navigating their journey. I talked about my patient navigator experience and how much he had helped me and how I wanted to give back to other patients with the same knowledge and understanding that I had received. They both thanked me and told me they had a few more interviews to do and I should know by the end of next week. I shook their hands and left the room knowing I had given it my best shot, and if someone with more experience got the role, I could accept it knowing that a decision had been made based on what would be best for the patients.

The following week came, and I received a call informing me that I had been chosen for the patient navigator rotational role. I was beyond ecstatic! They told me the role would be for six months and that I would have to undergo a six-week clinical training program centered on the product that I was supporting. This was no problem for me, as I loved to learn, and learning about a product that our company manufactured made it that more interesting.

During my training, I learned so much about the product and what is expected of the patients, including all the side effects they may experience. It was an infusion drug that took four to six hours from start to finish and was administered to the patient every six months. I could sympathize with the four to six infusion hours as my infusions had taken that long. It became apparent to me that I could make a difference in these patients' lives, as I had firsthand knowledge of being infused and had experienced a life-threatening disease. I would be able to provide guidance and help them through the kingdom of the sick.

The six weeks of training went by so quickly that before I knew it, I was calling my first patient. I let them know that I was their patient navigator and that I would be helping them through their treatment journey. The patients that I enjoyed the most were the new ones, as they had many questions about their treatment and the drug. I was only allowed to answer questions around the product, but for medical questions concerning their care, I would refer them to their doctor. But for questions like what they would do for the four to six hours in the infusion chair, I would share my experience and let them know what I had done to pass the time. There's something about knowing that someone has been through similar circumstances that brings comfort. They would thank me for sharing my story. I found it therapeutic, and they found it helpful. Another win-win situation.

My six-month rotation was an experience I would never forget. It brought solace during such a difficult time in my life. I also learned that a personal connection can be made with people suffering from different health issues, as we all are trying to find our way back to the kingdom of the well. I felt accomplished and fulfilled in my work as a patient navigator.

Continuing in that same vein of gratitude, there was a callout on our company's internal website to submit a story of why you thought the company was a great place to work. I read the submissions that had been posted, and some mentioned our great 401K plan, our sabbaticals, and our competitive pay. While I do appreciate all those awesome benefits, I felt compelled to write about the people and how their drive and energy made this company a great place to work.

I shared my journey as a patient and a caregiver. I wrote about how sometimes we can get lost in the day-to-day redundancies of work and lose sight of the bigger picture—finding the cure to cancer. I wrote that as a cancer warrior, I was living proof that we were getting there. I wrote about the employees and their compassion for patients and how, at every level of the company, their passion for their work was felt. I let them know that it's truly the employees that make the company so great.

The next thing I knew, my story was featured on our internal website, but not for the reason I had written it. I intended it to be a supplement to the article on why our company is a great place to work. Instead, it was featured as its own story, which took me by surprise. About a month later, a writer for our company newspaper reached out to me, wanting to interview me for our quarterly newsletter, which is sent globally to all our affiliates. My story was soon picked up by our global internal website. It was the perfect platform for me to reach out and thank everyone at our company for all that they do for patients.

Before I knew it, I was being asked to speak at different department offsites as a patient speaker. I used to be the first to cry whenever a patient speaker would show up to tell their story about taking one of our products and how it changed their life, along with the lives of their family members and loved ones. Now it had come full circle, and I was one of those patient speakers. True to form, I would always break down and cry when I told my story, especially when I would talk about my mom passing away and the struggles my dad went through. It never got easier, but as I looked up while delivering my talk, there wasn't a dry eye in the room. I was given so many great opportunities to say thank you to a company that had helped me through such a dark time in my life.

One of my favorite speaking engagements was when I was invited to speak at the manufacturing site for the drug that I took for my chemotherapy treatments. The site was in Florence, South Carolina, and that southern charm was on display—everyone was so welcoming. I was given a tour of their beautiful facility where my drug had been made, and I was able to meet the people who manufactured it. I couldn't thank them enough for all they do for cancer patients, and again, when I was delivering my talk, there wasn't a dry eye in the building. After the meeting, there was a reception, and I was looking forward to it, as I wanted to gauge why they were crying. I knew it was a sad story, but I wasn't looking for sympathy. My main purpose had been to thank them and let them know how important their work was for cancer warriors and their families. Because of them, my dad and I were able to take back our lives from this terrible disease.

At the reception, a lot of the employees came up to thank me for telling my story, and I wish I could have spoken with all of them. A few people told me about either their personal struggle with disease or a loved one's battle with cancer. It's so true that cancer not only affects the person with the disease, but also their loved ones. But there is something about the human connection and sharing your own personal story that makes life's hardships bearable. I would ask them what made them cry about my story, and they would respond that it was very inspirational.

I was surprised. Inspiration wasn't exactly the message I was trying to convey, and it left me speechless. I had simply wanted to thank them for all that they do. It made me realize that inspiration comes in many forms. The dictionary states that inspiration means "to fill (someone) with the urge or ability to do or feel something, especially to do something creative." Those people were an inspiration to me, as I had taken on the patient navigator role and these speaking engagements as a way of expressing myself and my gratitude. I just couldn't see how I was an inspiration to *them*, as I viewed my whole struggle with this disease as a hot mess, just doing what I had to do with bold action. No one is really prepared to receive a diagnosis of cancer, then soon after prepare a parent to go through their own journey, and then have the rock of your family pass away all at the same time. I never really thought of my story as inspirational, and I still don't. I just see it as dealing with the cards life dealt me and wanting to thank those who were able to assist me along the way and, in turn, "pay it forward." Also, besides showing my gratitude, what I also felt compelled to accomplish by telling my story was to provide hope to those who may need it, foremost being cancer warriors. I wanted to inject hope around the dark circumstances they may encounter in their journey. I left South Carolina feeling renewed and will always remember that Southern hospitality that I received.

Back at home, and still on a high from my trip, I received a call from our corporate relations department asking if it would be OK for them to share my story with an undisclosed vendor. They said that my story may help some patients who are currently being treated for cancer. I thought it was a little strange that they didn't share who the vendor was, but hey, if my story could help someone going through their journey, so be it. I wanted to help. I let them know that it would be OK and told them that I was open to speaking to the vendor if that would be easier. They said they would pass along the information and thanked me for my openness.

A few days later, I received an exciting follow-up call from them, letting me know that the vendor had really liked my story and that they wanted to film me for the next *Stand Up to Cancer* telecast to be aired in September 2018. I was honored! *Stand Up to Cancer* (SU2C) is a charitable program of the Entertainment Industry Foundation. It's an organization founded by women, and one of the founders was Katie Couric. I remembered following her journey as her late husband lost his battle to colon cancer. SU2C aims to raise significant funds for cancer research through online and televised efforts.

With this call, so many emotions came over me, and although I was honored to be a part of the telecast, I had a few questions, and I began asking myself, "Was I ready for this? Was I ready to own my journey on a national platform?"

Then I reflected. I remembered watching the 2016 *Stand Up to Cancer* telecast with excitement and awe. That was the year I received my "no evidence of disease," so it was special to me. The telecast was a one-hour special that aired on more than sixty broadcast and cable networks and streaming channels in the United States and Canada. I purchased my first SU2C t-shirt while watching the telecast to show my support. During the broadcast, cancer patients talk about their dream team, who they would want by their side during this difficult time.

I reflected on my own support system—my family, friends, and colleagues—who had all helped me carry the load. My doctors, oncologists, surgeons, and gastroenterologists, without whose scientific expertise, I wouldn't be here today. I thought about the patients I had seen speak about their journeys and how I cheered for them to keep going, as I knew those dark days wouldn't last forever. I knew exactly how they felt and thought they were brave to use this platform to raise funds for cancer research. So despite all my fears and anxiety, I excitedly accepted their invitation to film and attend the live telecast in September 2018.

My mom had been an avid Katie Couric fan and had followed her career. She had watched all her journalistic news shows, and the *Today* show, which Katie co-anchored, was, by far, her favorite morning show. Every now and then, she would update me with the going-ons in the world by starting it off with, "Do you know what Katie said today?" Katie's late husband, Jay Monahan, passed away from colon cancer in 1998. It was my same diagnosis, so when SU2C reached out to me, it spoke to me and hit home.

Once I accepted the invitation, I received an e-mail from Renee and Amanda at SU2C, letting me know how excited they were to meet me and explained that the segment I would be in would be called "Everyday Heroes." The piece would include everyday moments in my life, from my jog in the morning to having a quick breakfast with Jett and Cisco before work and then ending at my job with my coworkers. Although being in a segment called "Everyday Heroes" sounded a little presumptuous to me, the everyday moments in my life sounded easy enough to film.

After many phone calls and e-mails, I finally was able to meet Renee and Amanda the day before filming. They were just as nice in person as they had been over the phone and in their e-mails, and they made me feel comfortable with the process. As filming day drew closer, I was getting nervous and was glad they were there to provide support, along with a lot of laughs. I remember being so nervous right before filming my first scene, and I guess they could tell because Renee asked me if I was OK. I turned to her and said, "I'm OK, but a little nervous."

She looked me up and down and said, "Girl, you beat cancer . . . you can't be scared of this little camera!"

Amanda gave me a pat on the back, and we just started laughing. They knew how to put me at ease. It set the tone for the rest of the day, laughing while filming and with that...it was a wrap!

A few months passed, and before we knew it, it was the week of the telecast. The organization flew Cisco and me down to Los Angeles. Jett was already in Los Angeles, attending his first semester in college, and it also happened to be Jett's birthday weekend, so it couldn't have been more perfect. It was a special eighteenth birthday for him, hobnobbing with the stars. The night before the telecast, Cisco and I took Jett out to celebrate at a restaurant on the Santa Monica Pier. It was such a special night, celebrating his birthday and life in general. We walked to the end of the pier and watched the most beautiful sunset over the Pacific Ocean before returning to the hotel to get rest for the next day's big event.

The 2018 telecast aired live from The Barker Hangar in Santa Monica on Friday, September 7, 2018. It was shown on more than seventy broadcast and cable networks, as well as streaming and social platforms, including CBS, HBO, and NBC. It was made available to more than 190 countries. I was a little nervous as they told me I would walk onto the stage live, along with the other five everyday heroes, who I was able to meet and spend time with prior to and during our rehearsal time. They were such friendly people with amazing stories that showcased their strength and resilience through life's adversities and this terrible disease.

During our rehearsal, my family and I were escorted into the Barker Hangar, along with the five other "everyday heroes" and their families, via a backstage route to the main stage. It was dark as they led us through a maze of equipment, and we stepped carefully over cables and wires. Immediately after our final turn to the stage area, our eyes lit up with astonishment as we gazed upon the massive, bright stage lit up with the *Stand Up to Cancer* logo. As we turned around to take in the entire hangar, all we saw were empty stadium seats. They led up all the way up to the top of the hangar, and we were told that they would all be filled, including a standing-room-only section. Jett, Cisco, and the families of the other everyday heroes were escorted to the first row of the stadium seats, and the rest of us were ushered to the front of the stage and told that rehearsals had already started. As we approached the stage, a voice filled the entire hangar and said, "Please welcome Katie Couric." I was awestruck as we watched her approach the stage, and I smiled as I thought about my mom and how she used to watch all her shows. During her practice takes, she would look over at us and smile and wave. Anxiously, we all smiled and waved back. We were also lucky enough to see Little Big Town, a country music group, practice their set. As they were escorted off the stage, we were escorted onto the stage and shown our marks on the floor where we were to stand on the stage. Seemed easy enough, but once on the stage and looking up at the empty stadium seats and picturing it filled with people, I thought, *I hope I don't fall in front of all these people on an international broadcast.*

Once our rehearsal ended, Jett, Cisco, and I were shown into the VIP tent, which was set up right behind the hangar. As we walked the short distance from the hangar to the white tent, we were starstruck at every turn and looked at each other and said, "Hey, wasn't that . . . ?" as we saw Marlon Wayans, Mark Harmon, and David Spade walk by. In the tent, there was a party atmosphere with tables of appetizers lined up, passed hors d'oeuvres, and an open bar. As we walked through the crowded tent, wide-eyed, we saw a step and repeat banner with the Stand Up to Cancer logo on it for people attending the event to be photographed in front of. The photographer tapped me on my shoulder and said he wanted to photograph us. We were all smiles as we took our closeup together in front of the backdrop.

Before we knew it, we were ushered back into the hangar where we had front-row seats for all the action during the telecast. About twenty minutes into the show, I was escorted backstage, along with the five everyday heroes, and we were surprised to see Grammy Award Nominee Charlie Wilson enter the live stage first. Our video was shown while we were serenaded by Charlie Wilson singing "Stand Up for Something" accompanied by the group 4th Ave. Once again, we were all in awe as we watched them perform with our video as their backdrop. A few minutes before Charlie finished singing, our video was still playing, and we were invited on stage with Charlie Wilson and 4th Ave. It felt odd seeing actors, such as Matt Damon, Sofia Vergara, Maria Menounos, and Michael Ealy, in the audience as I was on stage. If you are interested in seeing the video, check it out on YouTube: "2018 Telecast Stand Up to Cancer." It will be at the 42:30 mark.

What a fulfilling night, celebrating my second anniversary in remission and Jett's eighteenth birthday in a way that gave back to help cancer warriors. We ended the night at the afterparty and made wonderful memories together! Yes, I had cancer, but cancer never had me!

CHAPTER 12

Every setback is a setup for a comeback! There were a lot of setbacks that we didn't see coming that my dad and I encountered along our cancer journey, but they were just the setups. I am happy to say that we have remained in remission for five years now and we are cancer-free. We no longer have to have scans or blood tests done multiple times a year—we were almost getting used to having those tests done all the time. Every quarter for the past five years, our peace of mind was restored, knowing that there was no evidence of disease from the results of scans and labs. We became almost dependent on those tests for the first few years, but as the years progressed, we became more confident about our health and more in tune with how our body felt, and so we became less and less dependent on those scans and tests. It was a liberating moment to know that we were free from those tests, and with our true warrior mentality, we embraced it— we aren't done yet with our comeback!

Our oncologists explained that we were now in the clear, and since it had been five years that we had been in remission, our scans would now be on a normal screening basis, typically every one to two years. It felt like chemo graduation all over again but even better. We were happy about not needing to have that iodine injected into us for the CT scans and being able to skip the multiple blood draws, but we also expressed our concern about stepping away from dependence on the scans. We were being told it was no longer needed, but would we feel just as safe and secure without all the now-routine follow-up appointments? Our doctors advised us that if we felt any discomfort to let them know, but there were no signs that concerned them, and we would be free to live our normal lives.

But normal, everyday life is very different post-cancer. Life would never be the same, but that's always not a bad thing. Post-cancer life taught me the true meaning of gratitude and how precious life is. My new normal now consists of appreciating every day given to me and knowing that tomorrow isn't promised. It brought a newfound appreciation of the past and a brand-new excitement for the future. Defeating colon cancer was a pretty big deal, and with the courage I gained, I gave myself permission to live my "new normal" in everyday life. I also have a greater respect and admiration for all healthcare workers and a deeper affinity for believing in science, all in tribute to those cancer warriors we have lost along the way.

For me, my journey of receiving a stage 3A colon cancer diagnosis, having surgery and then chemo treatments, unfolded at a rapid pace and I had no time to process my choices slowly. I was forced to deal with the current situation and wrap my head around decisions regarding those circumstances at a swift pace, whether it was dealing with my diagnosis to immediately going into colectomy surgery, followed quickly by chemotherapy, even from the stages of my mom passing away to two weeks later when my dad started his therapy seemed instantaneous. Quick decisions were made with confidence, backed by the trust I have in science. It made me realize that not all patients have the same confidence and support system that I had going through my treatments, and I wanted to assist them in any way I could. I found I could help by taking all the lessons of being a cancer warrior—good and bad—that I have learned and instill that same confidence in them by sharing my story. Even after my mom's passing, I was able to find joy again through the help of family and friends and was able to celebrate small accomplishments in life—just as my mother taught me. So yes, I will go back to normal life, but through the lens of a caregiver and patient recently returned from the kingdom of the sick to have happily regained her footing into the kingdom of the well.

During the summer of my fifth anniversary of being cancer-free, we went out to eat at a restaurant, and I saw a woman sitting at the table with her friends. I noticed that she was the only one at her table with a hoodie, jacket, and scarf on. She was also sipping a hot drink out of a mug. All her friends were wearing shorts and tank tops and drinking cold drinks, as it was a hot day in the Bay Area. It took me back, and I thought to myself, *That is exactly what I must have looked like a few years ago.* Then I thought, *I sure hope she doesn't have cancer,* and I said a silent prayer to bless her on her journey if that was the case. We bumped into each other in the restroom, and as she rolled up her sleeves to wash her hands, I saw the same bruises I had a few years ago. I had asked her politely if she was OK, and she half-smiled and replied that she was going through some type of treatment. I didn't pry anymore, as I have learned that some people don't like to share their story, but I did let her know that I went through something similar when I had cancer. I told her to keep fighting, as I know those tough days don't last forever. Her eyes started to well up with tears as she smiled, hugged me, and thanked me for my concern and for sharing my perspective. She said it was something she had needed in the moment. I guess this is what I mean by seeing things differently, those little observations that I wouldn't have noticed before I had cancer and being willing to act on them, making those small gestures. It's that club that I discussed earlier that no one wants to be a part of, but only members can truly understand.

For my dad, his treatments unfolded at a slower pace since he had a few months from his initial diagnosis to the start of his treatment plan. In those months, he had a lot of time to swirl and spin and question his confidence in himself and the science regarding his treatment. He had to deal with the loss of my mom on top of starting his treatments. It was a different path than mine, and I saw through his suffering how this disease can be so very harmful mentally and emotionally to cancer patients and caregivers. To combat the stress he was feeling, my brother and I reassured him that he was on the best possible treatment plan for his esophageal cancer. The pre-chemo appointments also relieved a lot of the stress he was feeling as the doctors were able to put him at ease by answering all his questions. Armed with the knowledge he gained from his doctors, his renewed faith in science and our support, he was resilient in his fight against cancer and, in time, was able to find joy and celebrate how far he has come on his own journey.

Shortly after my dad and I finished our last treatments, the side effects that we had experienced quickly started to subside, and we have no lasting adverse effects. Our lab reports quickly returned to within normal range, and physically, we were feeling fine. There are a few souvenirs from my time as a citizen of that other kingdom though—to this day, I prefer sipping out of a straw when drinking out of a metal cup or soda can. The harsh metallic taste in my mouth that I experienced when I was on the chemotherapy drugs was something that I can never forget. I also take light jackets with me everywhere I go, a holdover from my unbearable sensitivity to the cold during that time.

Looking back, the best part of my journey was being able to meet so many amazing people along the way. I was fortunate enough to be able to have some incredible doctors and nurses who were available to answer any questions and walk me through my treatment plans. All the appointments and information can be pretty daunting as a cancer patient, and my dad and I were lucky enough to have all our questions answered in a timely and compassionate way. Another amazing experience was connecting with patients who shared their personal stories and gave me their insight into the disease and treatments. Everyone has a story, and theirs will forever be imprinted on me. Their struggles are a true testament of strength and hope, and I am forever grateful. From the healthcare workers to patients themselves, all played a role in helping my dad and I get back to the kingdom of the well.

Although I lost my mom on my birthday during a difficult time in my life, I have learned to cope with her loss throughout the years. For the first couple of years, the hardest thing was trying to wrap my head around the sad idea that she lost her life exactly forty-five years after giving me life. Celebrating my birthday on the same day she lost hers just didn't seem right or fair, but as the years progressed, that date, July 19, has become more meaningful to me—it's bigger than just celebrating my birthday. It's a day we will forever share, where I reflect and celebrate what an incredible mother she was to my brother and me. It's a day that I thank her for instilling the key values that have helped me throughout my life.

The year 2016 will go down as the darkest year in my life, but in that deep darkness, you have to dig down deep to find your own light.

Sure, there will be bad years, but you just have to keep going and have hope, as there will also be amazing years ahead. Dr. Martin Luther King Jr. said it best, "Darkness cannot drive out darkness, only light can do that." That light brought me back to the kingdom of the well. That light from all the incredible people who shared their light with me—I am forever changed by it. It's a light I don't mind sharing with others.

The Covid-19 pandemic in 2020 marked my fifth anniversary of being cancer-free and in complete remission. Unfortunately, the pandemic sidelined my plans of celebrating with friends and family and going on a celebratory trip somewhere; however, what it brought me was something far greater than any trip or party. I had time to reflect on my time in both kingdoms, as well as the deep gratitude I have for my family and friends who helped me. My time in both kingdoms improved my ability to pivot during trying times and allowed me to find my deepest reserves of inner strength. Who knows what the future holds for me—truly, for any one of us—but I do know that every day brings new hope for better ones ahead. Cancer is just a chapter in my life. It altered it, but it didn't define me, for my true north runs deep in the values and beliefs with which I was raised. I truly believe it's not our circumstances that define us but how we choose to deal with those circumstances. Throughout my cancer battle, I was surrounded by the loving care of the family and friends who had helped me build my value system. They gave me every reminder I needed of how to play the hand I was dealt and to play to win.

I've tucked my passport to the kingdom of the sick away, in the hopes that it will never need to be used again. But every once in a while, I take a look through the stamps in it. Just as we hang on to our old passports to pull out of a drawer and flip through to see all the places we've been and remind us of our journeys, so it is with my passport to the kingdom of the sick. Those entry and exit stamps as a citizen during my own battle and the stamps as a visitor with my dad's journey help me reflect on the journey and remind me not to let the lessons I've learned and the experiences I've had in that kingdom be forgotten. It was a difficult journey, but in the end, it only fueled my love of life and helped me find my purpose—to help those in that kingdom.

CPSIA information can be obtained
at www.ICGtesting.com
Printed in the USA
BVHW071512011121
620453BV00006B/272